Coll

MW00629510

    Raised on a farm near Promontory Summit, Utah, Colleen was an outdoor gal from the moment she was born. Working and living in the outdoors is part of her heritage. Her grandparents came west as pioneers in covered wagons and her addiction to cooking with Dutch Ovens started at an early age. Her mother cooked many a meal in the farmhouse on a coal and wood stove. Her grandmother is quoted as saying "it is the healthiest kind of cookin' we can do for our families." With that heritage, a handwritten cookbook of old pioneer recipes, a father that was a Scoutmaster for 38 years, county fairs and 4H, you can see how her career as a mom who was a believer & loved life, an outdoor expert and master Dutch Oven cook came to be.

    Colleen loves to share knowledge and swap recipes with other Dutch oven fans, and in that pursuit teaches at the College of Southern Idaho and gives seminars at Sports Shows throughout the United States. In her spare time her love of the outdoors continues as she fishes, camps, and hunts with her 5 children, 9 grandchildren, and 5 great grandchildren. Colleen is the author of 7 books, loves to teach Dutch oven cooking, and with her history, good stories and funny anecdotes, brings warmth and laughter to each of her seminars. Like her Grandma and Mom used to say,

"Kissin' wears out, but cookin', don't."

5th Edition September 2012

INTRODUCTION

COLLEEN SLOAN	1
TABLE OF CONTENTS	2
ACKNOWLEDGMENTS	5
INTRODUCTION	7
SPENDING THE CONGRESSIONAL APPROPRIATIONS	8
MAP	9
COOKIN' FOR FUN WITH DUTCH OVEN	10
SEASONING YOUR DUTCH OVEN - NEVER INSIDE	11
CLEANING YOUR OVEN	12
STORING YOUR OVEN	13
TEMPERATURE GUIDE	14
COOK N DUTCH	15
STACKING DUTCH OVENS	16

THEN

MEMBERS OF THE EXPEDITION	17
FACTS ABOUT THE EXPEDITION	18
HOW WE SURVIVED - PORTABLE SOUP - POTAGES	20
BERRY SAUCE	21
BUFFALO JERKY BY THE CORPS OF DISCOVERY	22
CORN AND BEANS WITH DRIED NUT	23
TOMAHAWK HOMINY - FISH SOUP	24
WAPITI	25
KAMASS ROOT OR WILD HYACINTH (ALSO CALLED CAMAS)	26
SERGEANTS AND PRIVATES	27
LETTER FROM PRESIDENT THOMAS JEFFERSON	28
SOME SUGGESTED BOOKS TO ENJOY	32

MAIN RECIPES

WENDY'S BLACK POT DEER ROAST	33
BAKED BLACK POT DUCK	33
TURKEY STIR-FRY	34
YALLER BREAD WITH PINTOS	34
RANCH BEANS	35
FRY PAN OR SKILLET MEALS	36
ELK HOT DISH	36
SKILLET SPAGHETTI	36
LITTLE TWO-BIT CASSEROLE	37
MEATY CALICO BEANS	37
FRIENDSHIP MEAT PIE	38
LIMA'S AND SALT PORK	38
MOUTH WATERING PORK ROAST WITH VEGETABLES	39
HUNGRY BOY CASSEROLE	39
FOURTH OF JULY MEAT AND BEAN CASSEROLE	40
GARLIC SWISS STEAK	41
ORANGE CUBE STEAK OR CHICKEN	41
PORK CHOPS AND STUFFING	42
RODEO PORK WITH ONIONS	42
SWEET AND SOUR PORK	43
BEEF AND BEAN SKILLET SUPPER	43
ALA FAST POT ROAST	44
EASY POT ROAST	44
OUT OF THE CHUTES BEEF GOULASH	45
BEHIND THE CHUTES BEEF GOULASH	45
SALMON SURPRISE	46
CAMPERS STEW	46
ORNERY OLE CUSS STEW	47
CHUCK WAGON SKILLET SPAGHETTI	47
HOBO SURPRISE	48
HEAVENLY HAMBURGER PIES	48

Bunk House All Day Stew --- 49
Back Country Stew -- 49
Sweet and Sour Meat Balls -- 50
Stew Do in a Skillet --- 50
Roast Beef and Beans -- 51
Italian Broccoli and Chicken Supreme ----------------------------------- 51
Red Sauce Pork Chops --- 52
Enchiladas Dutch Oven Style -- 52
Steak Style Meat Loaf --- 53
Chimichangas --- 53
Jambalaya --- 54
Tamale Casserole -- 55
Bean Dip Chili -- 55
Glazed Ham steak -- 55
No-Fuss Chicken --- 56
Sweet and Sour Pork Kabobs -- 56
Lamb and Rice Skillet Dinner -- 57
Lamb with Zucchini and Macaroni --------------------------------------- 57
Lamb & Eggplant Stew -- 58
List of Civilians on the Expedition -------------------------------------- 58
Dutch Oven Salmon in Puff Pastry --------------------------------------- 59
Deviled Eggs -- 60
Herb's Salmon or Tuna Bake --- 60
Little Porky --- 61
Marinated Halibut Steaks -- 61
Irish Fish Steaks --- 62
Irish Stuffed Fish --- 62
Salmon Surprise -- 62
Okie Dokie Sliced Baked Potatoes -------------------------------------- 63
Dove and Rice Casserole -- 63
Quail on the Green --- 64
Holiday Pork Chops--- 64

BREADS AND DESSERTS

All Purpose Baking Mix -- 65
Banana Chocolate Nut Bread -- 65
Apple Crisp --- 66
Blackberry Cobbler -- 66
Quick Lemon-Walnut Treat -- 67
Easy Sponge Cake --- 68
Mississippi Mud Cake -- 69
Indian Charlie's Pudding --- 70
Homemade Yeast --- 70
Chinese Chocolate Drops -- 71
Peppermint Gumdrops -- 71
Chocolate Peanut Candy --- 72
Pecan Logs --- 72
Log Cabin Sugar Cream Pies -- 73
Sausage Apple Pastry Puffs --- 74
Honey Berry Shortcakes --- 74
Double-Decker Confetti Brownies --------------------------------------- 75
Blueberry Streusel Cobbler --- 75
Blueberry Streusel Pound Cake --- 76
Streusel --- 76
Pumpkin Pecan Cake --- 77
... Filling/Topping -- 77
Cranberry Orange Pound Cake --- 78
Vanilla Butter Sauce --- 78
Peanut Butter Chocolate Cake -- 79
Glazed Lemon Cake -- 79
Shredded Wheat Bread - 2 Loaves -------------------------------------- 80
Sheepherders Bread --- 80
Onion Crescent Roll Bread -- 81
The Easy Dinner Roll --- 81

QUICK BEER BREAD RECIPE -- 82
BISCUITS -- 82
EASY INDIAN FRY BREAD --- 82
SPOON BREAD --- 83
SOURDOUGH STARTER --- 83
POTATO SOUR DOUGH STARTER --- 84
SOURDOUGH POTATO DOUGHNUTS -- 85
SOURDOUGH RANGER BISCUITS --- 86
BEER BREAD ALA DUTCH -- 86
CORNMEAL BISCUITS --- 87
CHEESE ROLLS ON THE DOUBLE -- 87
AUNT LIZZIES BEER BREAD --- 88
COWBOY APPLE PIE -- 88
BANDIT BEER BUNS -- 89
IRISH BROWNIE PIE -- 89
APPLE PIE CAKE -- 90
SNOWFLAKE COBBLER --- 90
PRAIRIE DEEP DISH APPLE PIE --- 91
THE GREATEST RHUBARB CAKE YOU EVER ATE -------------------------------------- 91
CARROT PINEAPPLE CAKE --- 92
FRESH RASPBERRY PEACH PIE --- 93
CHOCOLATE LOVERS DELIGHT -- 94
DUTCH APPLE CRISP --- 94
CHERRY CHOCOLATE SURPRISE CAKE -- 95
EASY PEACH COBBLER -- 95
SOURDOUGH OATMEAL BREAD --- 96

MISCELLANEOUS

ACE CAJUN MUSHROOMS --- 97
HONEY ONIONS -- 97
BACON CARROTS --- 98
CABBAGE AND TOMATO SOUP --- 98
CALICO BEANS -- 99
CARROT PUDDING -- 99
UPTOWN GREEN BEANS -- 100
COUNTRY STUFFED MUSHROOMS --- 100
LEMON "OH MY GOSH" PUDDING CAKE --- 100
COWGIRL APPLE PIE CAKE -- 101
CORNMEAL CORN DISH -- 101
SPORTSMAN BAKED BEANS --- 102
HOME STYLE CHICKEN POT PIE -- 102
COUNTRY DUMPLINGS --- 103
SAUSAGE DIP --- 103
TERRIBLY TASTY TARTER SAUCE --- 103
CHEESY MUSTARD SAUCE -- 103
CREAMY HOMEMADE MUSHROOM SOUP --- 104
MEAT BASTING SAUCE -- 104
RED ITALIAN SAUCE --- 104
PEANUT BUTTER BAR-B-QUE SAUCE --- 105
BARBEQUE SAUCE BY JACK -- 105
DUTCH OVEN SAUSAGE SOUFFLÉ -- 106
CHILI ONION SOUP -- 107
JERKY --- 107
EGG DROP SOUP --- 108
OLD WOODSTOVE BAKED BEANS --- 108
BITE SIZE APPETIZERS -- 109
HONEY SWEET AND SOUR -- 109
ZUCCHINI SCRAMBLE --- 109
SPANISH LEFT OVER POTATOES -- 109
OZARK BAKED CORN -- 110
CHILI EGG PUFF -- 110
BOURBON BARBECUED CHICKEN --- 111
BEST EVER RUM CAKE -- 111
NOTES --- 112

Acknowledgments

They say that History repeats itself, and if that's true, I want to be part of the Lewis and Clark Expedition of Tomorrow. When I first met Florence and Ann at Magpie Books in Three Forks, Montana I didn't even know what the significance of "The Head Waters of the Missouri" meant. Florence took me out to the Park and I was hooked. She fell for me and I fell for the History of Lewis and Clark. As I stood there on the bluff, I realized I could be standing on the same exact soil that the Corps of Discovery stood on. Florence and Ann suggested the book of "Undaunted Courage" by Steven Ambrose and my curiosity became genuine interest. My friends Gene and Holly Griswold came into the picture when I was cooking for the restoration of the old OTO Dude Ranch in Montana. I asked him a couple of questions about the trail that goes by his home near Hood River, Oregon. He knew so much, had read the journals, assisted in looking for the trail, and had a truly genuine interest in the historical value of the trek. Gene offered his research abilities and talked to me many hours on the phone to help me with questions about the food they ate, how they prepared it and the marvelous contribution that Sacajawea made to the success of the trip. And now, to all of you who have listened to me tell of the things I've discovered and shared the excitement I feel about Lewis and Clarks place in History, **I THANK YOU**. I need to thank Camp Chef for believing in me and asking for my help with the Lewis and Clark Project of Cast Iron Commemoratives. My friends at the Nine Mile Ranger station near Missoula Mt., my second home, Milo and Walt for listening and offering all they could about the trail and the work they had done on it. To my family and my Larry----I think we've done it again.

You got a happy Cowgirl on your hands.

This book is full of historical facts and the following credits need to be issued. The Journals by Bernard DeVoto make you feel as though you were there. Traveling the Lewis and Clark Trail by Julie Fanselow gives you great ideas of places to see and roads to get there. The Incredible Journey of Lewis & Clark by Rhoda Blumberg. The truth about Sacajawea by Kenneth Thomasma, The Journals of Patrick Gass, Dr. Gary Moulton (my HERO) from the University of Nebraska, and many more.

Sacagawea "sah KAH guh WEE uh",

(1787?-1812),

was a Shoshone Indian woman who accompanied the Lewis and Clark expedition in 1805 and 1806. The expedition; an early exploration of the Northwestern United States was led by U.S. Army officers Meriwether Lewis and William Clark. Sacagawea has often been depicted in art and literature as the expedition's heroic guide. But in reality, her contributions, though important, were much more limited. Sacagawea's name means Bird Woman. It is also spelled Sacajawea "SAK uh juh WEE uh" or Sakakawea "sah KAH kah WEE uh".

◆ **In 1978,**

◆ Congress established the Historic Trail for all of us to learn more about our history and I hope this book will spark some interest for you and your family. Take a vacation and explore some of the trail sites. Stand on the hill above the Head Waters and see what they saw. Feel the spirit of the men as they saw the awesome Rockies that they must cross. Visit Pompeys Pillar near Billings, Mont. or canoe the Missouri for a taste of history. Go to Ft. Mandan, or Ft. Clatsop and feel their presence and marvel at their survival knowledge. One of the greatest feats of history is there for you and your family to discover. Just like they did only 200 years later. You won't be sorry. The Corps of Discovery was on the trail from May 14, 1804 to Sept. 23, 1806. They traveled over 8000 miles and camped in over 700 campsites. There is physical evidence in only two or three of those sites. They were the original "No Trace" campers. The journals tell approximately where they were, but no physical evidence can be found. Most people had given them up for dead, but President Jefferson held out hope that they would return. What a marvelous journey, so full of stories and experiences better than any author could imagine.

Be part of history, and travel the trail for a wonderful experience in American History.

Introduction

"We Proceeded On." You read that throughout the Journals. What a statement to reflect on. As I read the Journals I became intrigued by the food preparation and the foods they ate. Their diet didn't seem very versatile or healthy. The men ate an average of 9 pounds of meat everyday, when it was available. They burned a lot of calories and protein with the amount of energy they expended daily. I decided it would be educational and interesting to learn more about how they prepared food and from what sources it came.

Today we grab a map and plan a vacation by car, plane, bus or train and never think about it. We know where we are going, or we ask someone directions. After Lewis and Clark left the St. Louis area, they relied on what information they gathered from trappers and traders of the area. They gathered more info from the Native Americans as they passed through their territories. When they reached the Headwaters, it was unmarked and unknown territory. Sacajawea became a valuable source of information when she began to recognize familiar sites from her childhood travels with her people. The Beaver head rock, The Buffalo rock canyon, and Camp Fortunate, near Dillon, on I-15.

The Expedition was a dream of Pres. Thomas Jefferson who had a fascination for the lore of the west since his childhood. Congress appropriated $2500.00 for the trip, which actually ended up costing about $38,000.00 dollars. They logged over 8000 miles, Paddling, Walking, and Horseback riding. They left the New Americas after the Missouri river and crossed the Continental Divide. They entered the Oregon Territories, which were later annexed, into the USA. This was one of the most important investments the American Congress ever made. Never has an event changed or influenced a nation in the way the "Corps of Discovery " did. Jefferson never put the job out for bid; he just knew that his lifetime friend, Meriwether Lewis was the right man.

Spending the Congressional appropriations from Congress

Planning a 3-day camping trip today takes a lot of thought. Imagine planning for an undetermined amount of time & no supermarkets to shop in. The food alone for the trip weighed over 7 tons. The $2500.00 appropriated by Congress was spent as follows:

Mathematical Instruments	$ 217.00
Provisions (portable soup, molasses, sugar, salt, pots & black kettles, side pork whiskey & etc.)	$ 244.00
Material for portable packs	$ 55.00
Pay or wages for Hunters, Guides and Interpreters	$ 300.00
Pay for members moving expenses	$ 100.00
Weapons and Guns	$ 81.00
Camp equipment	$ 255.00
Medical supplies	$ 55.00
Boats	$ 430.00
Contingencies	$ 87.00
Indian gifts & presents (475 yards of red flannel, 12 doz. Pocket mirrors, 73 bunches of beads, 2800 fish hooks & 4600 needles)	$ 696.00

Then as now, it was hard for the US to stay within its budget. They were already over budget and ultimately the total cost of the expedition would go over $38,000.00. Lewis carried a letter of credit from President Jefferson, which made up the difference

During the journey of the Corps of discovery, President Thomas Jefferson instructed both Lewis and Clark to keep daily journals or logs of their trip. The written Journals are public knowledge and have been condensed and rewritten by several people. The Corps of Discovery made use of the available foods that were along the trail. Lewis had purchased 193 lbs. of portable soup for the trip, but saved that for times when the daily hunts were not successful.

Lewis and Clark

May 14, 1804
To
Sept. 23, 1806

Started
and
Ended
near

St. Louis, Mo.

They
Traveled
over
8000
Miles by
land and
water

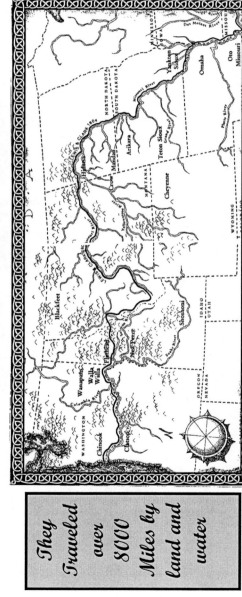

This map represents the trail traveled by the Corps of Discovery.

This peace medal was designed by President Jefferson and hung on ribbons. They were presented to most Chiefs along the way.

COOKIN' FOR FUN WITH DUTCH OVEN

I guess from the very beginning, I have been a Dutch oven fan. I actually got started with my dad and mom because they were both great cooks. My Great Grandparents came across the plains with the covered wagons and brought Black pots with them. My dad was in Scouting for 38 years and Dutch oven cooking has been a standard for scout cooking because of its versatility. It just wouldn't seem right not to have Stew or Chili in a Dutch oven for winter camp.

The Dutch oven like the Indian was pushed into a back corner by our advancing civilization. Whenever anyone came upon one, Grandma knew what it was and basically how to use one. Though mostly forgotten. The Dutch oven is rich in American history and tradition. Whenever a Mountain man or Prospector was around you would usually see one hanging from the packhorse. Trail drives and Chuck Wagons were always equipped with several. It made sense to cook with one, cause the lid kept the dust out and the heavy Pot would not blow over. Even Lewis and Clark carried black kettles.

Although they have changed in size, looks and even lost their legs, in some cases they are still as useful as ever and the briquettes have made them easier to use and more inventive in gourmet cooking. If you ever get the chance to attend a Cook-off sponsored by the International Dutch Oven Society, you'll taste some of the best food ever to cross your tongue. You can't help but go back for seconds.

SEASONING YOUR DUTCH OVEN --------NEVER INSIDE

Throw away the instructions.

If you ask 100 People how to season a Dutch oven, you'll probably get 15 different answers. Most Dutch ovens today are coated with a Protective substance by the manufacturer, usually wax, and all you need do is heat your oven and the wax will turn to a liquid. Wipe it out with a paper towel and oil the inside. You can also let the wax burn out. When it quits smoking you can oil it and put it outside on a Barbecue at medium heat for a propane stove or on 25 to 30 briquettes in the Collapsible stove or the Volcano until it turns black. This bakes a protective grease coating into the Pot and virtually gives your Pot a Teflon like finish. I always turn my Dutch ovens upside down so no grease will Puddle in the bottom.

If your Pot is seasoned well and used often, you will find it very easy to clean. If your Pots are cleaned while they are hot, they can be wiped out with VINEGAR water with virtually no scraping. The handy little pot scraper is an added bonus when cleaning Dutch ovens. I mix my Vinegar 1 Part Vinegar to 4 Parts Water and keep it in a spray bottle in my food box so I will have it every where I go. Vinegar is a great disinfectant and a natural Tenderizer for all foods. After most dishes, you should be able to wipe a Dutch oven out with a paper towel to clean it. Any oil or shortening will do for seasoning. I recommend using Bacon grease, Lard, vegetable oil or white solid shortening. These are the lowest flash point oils on the market.

Remember that the only way to dry cast iron is to return the pot to the heat and evaporate the moisture.

CLEANING YOUR OVEN

A lot of people will tell you never to wash the inside of your Pot with soap, but I have found on occasion that I have had to. I have a Pot of my Dads that is 55 years old and it has been washed several times. It has no legs and today still cooks as good as any of my brand new ones. These Pots are not fragile, but still require a certain amount of care. Dropping them or banging them against a hard surface could crack them and then their ability to hold the hot moisture that cooks your food is gone.

When you wash a cast iron pot, use only a mild detergent and always rinse it thoroughly with hot water to release the soap from the seasoning. Always heat your pan thoroughly after each use, to dry out the moisture before storing it. I always clean my pans hot because it helps to release the food particles. I find it helpful to return the Pot to the heat after emptying it, and spraying in a little vinegar water to soften the food. Then I wipe it clean with paper towels, heat and allow it to cool down, before storing the Pots in a dry Place with a clean paper towel inside to keep the moisture from rusting the surface. You take care of them and they'll do you proud. The 1 Part vinegar & 4 Parts water is a great cleaning agent and disinfectant. The use of Apple Cider Vinegar is something I learned from my Pioneer Grandparents and my Mom.

It is not necessary to oil your oven before putting it away, but if you do, be sure to wipe it out thoroughly with a Paper towel to avoid rancid oil build up.

Your dutch oven will be your best friend if you use it properly.

Storing your Oven

When storing your oven, be sure that you place a couple paper towels inside, to make sure that any moisture that formed will be absorbed by the paper towel. If rust forms in your Pot, simply scour it out with an SOS type Pad and rinse it thoroughly with hot water, dry, and re-season it before you use it again. As you cook with it you will automatically re-season it each time. If you store your ovens after heating them to dry them out, with out oiling them, you will never have to worry about rancid oil. If you use too much oil and it becomes rancid it will be easily detected by the spoiled smell of the Pot when opened. The grease actually goes rather yellow-orange, looks like a gummy texture. Simply fill your oven with water, add a cup of apple cider Vinegar and boil for 1/2 hour on the stove. Pour out the water. You should be able to scrape or scour out the rancid grease. Rinse well, dry and then lightly re-season while it is hot. Do this out side on a propane or briquette barbecue.

Be sure to heat your Pot and lightly grease it before you use it again. If you have the storage bags they are nice to keep your ovens clean.

If your oven gets real rusty, you could try sand blasting, soaking it in coke, scouring with SOS for surface rust, or soaking it in hay and 1 cup of apple cider vinegar and enough water to cover the inside. Just look in the yellow Pages of your phone book under sand blasting. Everyone has their secret and you need to Practice with your oven and do what suits you best. The more you try the better it will get. Like Mama used to say:

"Practice will make Perfection Happen".

JUDGING THE RIGHT TEMPERATURE

BAKING: When using the Black Pot to bake in, the heat must be distributed on the top and bottom to maintain the proper temperature. Usually a 350 to 375 degree temperature is sufficient to bake most any dish. If you are outside in the wind it will take away some of your heat, but the following Chart should help. You can raise or lower the temperature by adding 1 briquette for every 18 to 20 degrees you wish to add to the cooking temperature.

Oven Size (in inches)	8"	10"	12"	14"	16"	22"
Top Coals	11	13	15	17	19	25
Oven Size +3						

In your Volcano or collapsible stove, 12 Briquettes with no top heat will keep your oven at 350 to 375 degrees. Use the damper (Control ring) to control the burning rate.

Oven Size	8"	10"	12"	14"	16"	22"
Bottom Heat	6	8	10	12	14	20
Oven size - 2						

Arranging the briquettes so that the heat remains even is also very important. Place your coals in a circle underneath and on top. Never place coals in the middle underneath. Baking can be a lot of fun in a Dutch oven but proper heat is important. The smell will tell you when it's done. You can time it if you wish. Lifting the lid will add extra time to the cooking. Use a good name brand of briquettes for a more even heat. Briquettes are a great storage fuel because they don't evaporate or gel up.

COOK N DUTCH

If ever the Old West would come to your mind, just Pull out the old black Pot and hang it over the campfire on a tripod. Smell the smoke of a thousand campfires and picture the Pioneer women preparing a one Pot supper after a long days walk. Hear the cowboys humming a tune as they wait for the camp cook to holler, "Come and Get it". Lids off! The smell of Campfire Beans with Side Pork, and Sour Dough Dutch oven Bread makes your mouth water. The name DUTCH OVEN is used quite loosely. It actually applies to any cast iron pot with a lid on it. The bottom is flat, and it may or may not have legs. My first Pot did not have legs, but now, most of them do.

Top   Bottom

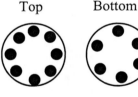

Always more heat on top than on the bottom when cooking with Briquettes only

Charcoal Placement

Your DUTCH OVEN will serve you well if you take <u>proper care</u> of it and treat it <u>with respect</u>.

STACKING DUTCH OVENS

Stacking the Dutch Ovens will depend on how many you intend to feed and if you are going to prepare more than a one dish meal. Stacking saves on briquettes but the cooking time of each oven is also important. Your roast or spareribs may need 2 hours and bread only 45 minutes. Wind will have a tendency to make the briquettes burn hotter. Damp weather will make your briquettes burn slower and put out less heat. Keep the briquettes off the wet ground. A simple fire blanket or foil will accomplish this. Simple tin foil wrapped around 3 sticks in the ground can help to divert the wind. Be sure to replenish your heat source when needed. The average size briquette lasts at full heat value for 25 to 30 minutes. On the previous page I have given you a simple formula for unexpected company. I hope you can enjoy the recipes that follow and will try some of your own. If you should invent a new recipe I'd love to hear from you. Sharing Dutch oven fun is what makes the Oven cookin appear to be so friendly.

♦ The 15-star American flag was the one carried by the Corp of discovery. They carried 3 different sizes. A large one was flown over the forts and major camps. The rest were given to selected Indian leaders as emblems of peace and to represent a bond of peace between the tribes and the new nation.

Lewis and Clark Corps of D' Discovery Cookbook

Where
they got it!

What they
learned!

(1803 - 2003)

LEWIS & CLARK
CORP OF DISCOVERY

1806 · 2006

Then

What they
Ate!

How they
fixed it!

How it all Began

Thomas Jefferson - Born April 14th, 1743
-----Died July 4th 1826

He was the third president of the United States of America and the man with the vision of a nation from sea to shining sea. The first conversation known about the expedition was in 1793 recorded between Thomas Jefferson and George Rogers Clark, the Elder brother of William Clark. Jefferson expressed his desire to organize an expedition to explore the Missouri river west. He was turned down 3 or 4 times for the funding.

Members of the expedition

Meriwether Lewis - Born August 18th, 1774
---Died October 11th, 1809

Lifetime friend to Thomas Jefferson, he was appointed to Secretary of State in 1801. Thomas Jefferson told Lewis of his fascination with the west. In 1802, Lewis agreed to take charge of the expedition with the condition that William Clark becomes his 2nd in command. Clark accepted in April of 1803. Lewis took his Newfoundland dog "SEAMAN" with him to the west coast and back.

William Clark - Born August 1st, 1770
---Died September 1st, 1838

Clark was at one time a commander over Lewis in the Army. Lewis had great respect for him. Clark brought his lifetime black servant "YORK" with him on the expedition. Clark earned the reputation of "THE REDHEAD". He was well respected by the Indians. He finally earned the rank of Captain from Congress in April 2000. Lewis and Clark were real American heroes. It doesn't matter what they went to find. They PROCEEDED ON to find more than Thomas Jefferson had ever dreamed.

FACTS ABOUT THE EXPEDITION

1. During the entire trip, only one man died. No one knows for sure, but it is believed it was from appendicitis. Sergeant Charles Floyd.

2. Members of the Corps suffered injuries, illnesses, infections, axe gashes, dislocated shoulders boils and only one single gunshot wound.

3. The journals briefly mentioned a re-occurring disease and fever that Sacagawea had. She almost died but Lewis saved her. She died years after the expedition on December 20th, 1812 in Fort Manuel, So. Dakota.

4. She carried a baby on her back for over 6000 miles. She was the only woman to make the trip. Her presence was a sign of a peaceful mission. More than once she saved the lives of the men from the Indians.

5. Lewis received the only gunshot wound. Private Cruzatte shot Lewis in the hip while out hunting. An accident, the 1st hunting accident reported, but never admitted to by Cruzatte.

6. The grizzly bear was new to the Corps. William Clark was the 1st to see one. He wounded it but it got away. The 1st grizzly killed was by Lewis and Cruzatte on April 29th, 1805.

7. Jean Babtiste was the only baby to make the trip. Nick named "POMP" by Clark. Born to Sacagawea at Fort Mandan in North Dakota. William Clark educated Jean after Sacagawea died. There is little known about Sacajawea's daughter Lizette, also raised by Clark.

8. Sacagawea discovered that the Chief of the Shoshoni Indians was her brother, Camewaite. This was one of the greatest favors the Corp received.

9. The Corps were the 1st Americans to erect a permanent flagpole west of the Missouri and the 1st Americans to celebrate the first 4th of July west of the Missouri.

10. The corps used their last whiskey to celebrate the 1st, 4th of July celebrated west of the Continental Divide. However, near the "John Day" river, in Oregon, Pvt. John Collins presented them with a kind of beer made from some Nez Perce bread that had fermented.

11. Captain Clark mentioned that he had carved his name in a tree near Ft. Canby state park, Oregon near the coast of the Pacific Ocean. No trace was ever found.

12. The Corps discovered 122 new species of animals, and 178 never before seen plants. Many samples of these were sent back to President Jefferson before they left Ft. Mandan.

13. After Lewis and Clark, no one ever reacted to the Indians like Lewis and Clark did. The Indians referred to St. Louis as "THE RED HEADS TOWN".

14. Unfortunately, no record was kept of the 1st meeting between Lewis and President Jefferson.

15. Lewis and Clark traveled more miles in Montana than any other state.

♦ Monday May the 14, 1804. Showery day. Captain Clark set out at 3 o'clock P.M. for the western expedition. One gun fired. A number of Citizens see us Start. The party consisted of 3 Sergeants and 38 good hands. We sailed up the Missouri 6 miles and encamped. Sergeant John Ordway's first journal entry.

HOW WE SURVIVED

We know from the journals that the Corp ate a variety of foods. Foods they brought with them, foods they obtained by hunting and fishing, and foods they traded for and received from the Native Americans.

Lewis noted that he had bought 193 lbs. of "portable soup" from Francois Baillet, a cook in Philadelphia. Portable soup was either a dry bouillon or a thick liquid-type substance made from beef and stored in tins for the expedition. Heating water and dissolving the bouillon was the usual way to eat it. Most of the men of the Corp did not like the soup and ate it only during the trip over the Bitterroot Mountains in Sept. of 1805. Basically, it's meat broth rendered down until it forms a gelatin.

PORTABLE SOUP

Williamsburg " Art of Cookery" 1729. Take a leg of veal, strip it of the skin and the fat, then take all the muscular or fleshy Parts from the bones; boil this flesh gently in such a quantity of water, and so long a time, till the liquor will make a strong jelly when its cold. This you may try by taking out a spoonful now and then, and letting it cool. In the late 1750's the Royal Navy began providing seaman with portable soup.

POTAGES;

Let beef or chicken soup get cold, skim off every particle of fat. Boil it until thick. Season very highly with pepper, salt, cloves and mace. Add a little brandy or wine, and pour it over platters not more than a quarter of an inch thick. Let it be until cold, and then cut in 2 or 3-inch thick squares. Set them in the sun to dry, turning often. Store them in airtight containers with papers in between. (You guessed it…early bouillon cubes!!!) **Portable soup** 1845.

Imagine trying to plan enough food to feed 33 people for an undetermined time and traveling into unknown territory. Learning to depend on the land was how Lewis and Clark decided to plan for food. Lewis took the essentials of the time with side pork, salt, portable soup, etc. This was for times when they couldn't kill enough fresh meat to survive on. The Corp actually ate an average of 9 lbs. of meat a day when available. Lewis relied on the expert marksmanship of his top hunters. Cruzatte, Clark, Gass, Lewis and York. Everyone carried rifles and brought in food but Cruzatte and Lewis did the most hunting.

The women of the Mandan and Hidatsa were expert farmers. They grew Corn, Squash and beans. They gathered roots, June berries, Sand cherries and grasses for flour. They pounded berries and seeds into their meats to dry for winter.

Sacajawea taught them to look for roots and other greens and grasses, but the Corp ate mostly meats. East of the Missouri, Buffalo, Elk, Deer and anything they shot they ate. West of the Mountains, Fish and roots were plentiful but the men preferred dog. They felt that the fish caused their illnesses and diarrhea. They traded for dogs, which they preferred over Horsemeat.

BERRY SAUCE

2 cups of water
2 handfuls of sugar or honey
1/4 cup Flour, ground from squash, corn, or
    sweet grasses.
3 cups fresh or dried berries
Pinch of salt when available

Combine all ingredients except the berries in a kettle and bring to a boil,
Simmer slowly until the mixture thickens.
    Serve over breads or meats.

"This being my 34th birthday I ordered a saddle of fat venison, an elk fleece and a beaver tail to be cooked and a desert of Cherries, plums, Rasberry currents and grapes of superior quality. This was the 1st Elk Killed on the expedition."
William Clark, August 1, 1804

List of the Foods they ate:

MEATS: Salted Pork, which they brought with them, Deer, Bear, Rabbit, Wolf, Elk, Beaver, Buffalo, Prairie Dog, Squirrel, Porcupine, Antelope, Dog, Otter, Badger, Mountain sheep, Mountain Goat, Cougar, Horse, Crawfish, Whale and Cabre, Pheasants, Swans, Ravens, Eagles, Turkey Buzzards, Quail, Vultures, Hawks and Pelicans. FISH: Catfish Salmon, Bass, Pike, Sunfish, Euchalon, Sturgeon, Anchovies and Crawfish. STARCHES: Flour-biscuits, Camas Root, Wapato Root, Thistle Roots, Uppah, Cous Cous, Shapaleel (Indian Bread). FRUITS: Dried apples, Mulberries, Grapes, Plums, Cherries, Calimous, Rabbit berries Persimmons, Gooseberry, Choke Cherry, Yellow, Red, and Black Currents, Strawberries, and Pawpaws. DRINKS: Taffia, (made from distilled coarse molasses), Brandy, Whiskey, and water.

BUFFALO JERKY

(by the Corp of Discovery)

Slice lean Buffalo meat into thin strips. Rub any available spices and Salt into the meat. Thread the meat strips onto sticks and dry over the campfire. If the meat was not dry, the men would tie the strips to the mast on the boats. After the winter of 1804, at Fort Mandan the Pirogues and keelboat were sent back to St. Louis so the meat had to be dried over campfires only. This cut the party to 4 civilians, 2 Captains, 3 Sergeants and 23 enlisted men.

The Army's contractor for rations, Major Rumsey, supplied 14 flour kegs, and 19 salted Pork legs. From the St. Louis area, Lewis purchased, 45 kegs of Salt Pork, 50 of flour, 18 of whiskey and seven of corn. They received what they tallied as 4175 complete rations at 14-1/2 cents per pound, 5555 rations of flour at 4-1/2 cents per pound, 25 casks of corn at 50 cents, 12 casks of salt, 100 gallons of whiskey, 4000 rations of pork at 4-1/2 cents, 1 keg of hogs lard, 1 bag of coffee, 50 weight, 2 ditto of sugar, 7 bags of biscuit, 4 barrels of biscuit, 44 kegs of pork packed with 3115,6 half barrels of pork ditto, weight 590. As you can see, they went with enough food to carry them thru the first 10 months knowing they would find fresh meat and trade for foods from the

Indians. They must have gained a wealth of knowledge from the Indians on the preparation of the food from the land. Oh how I wished I could have been there.

Lewis prepared a dish like this for Camewaite, Chief of the Shoshoni tribe. Sacajawea also gave her brother his first taste of sugar and squash. He said it was very tasty.

CORN AND BEANS WITH DRIED NUTS

3 spoonfuls of Lard
2 or 3 cups dried beans, hominy or roots
1 cube of portable soup
1 cup of nuts or seeds

Melt the lard in a cast iron pot, and add pinches of any flavorings you have. Add all remaining ingredients and simmer until cooked through. Serve with fresh seeds or nuts on top.

"Several horses slipped and rolled down steep hills which hurt them very much the one which carried my desk and small trunk Turned over and rolled down a mountain for 40 yards and lodged against a tree, broke the desk the horse escaped and appeared but little hurt Some others verry much hurt. When we arrived at the top as we conceved, we would find no water and Concluded to camp and make use of the snow we found on the top to cook the remns of our colt and make our supe, evening verry cold and cloudy nothing killed today except 2 phests. From this mtn. I could observe high rugged mountains in every direction as far as I could see"

William Clark, September 15, 1805

- The 1st buffalo were sighted in August 1804 near the middle of the Missouri river. This is near the borders of present day Iowa, Nebraska and South Dakota line.

- Millions of Buffalo grazed the plains in the early 1800's. Today less than 1000 Buffalo exist in the USA.

- The Corps crossed the Continental Divide 5 times! (3 going west, 2 going east)

- Lewis was the first American to record the crossing.

Tomahawk Hominy

The Indians used wood ash to make bread and hominy. Take 6 or 8 ears of corn and remove husks, wash and shell enough corn to make about 2 quarts. Add 4 quarts of cold water and 4 tbsp. fine wood ash (called saluratus and known today as refined baking soda). Soak for 10 to 12 hours. Bring the mixture to a boil in the soaking kettle. Cook for about 3 or 4 hours till hulls loosen. Add more water as they cook to keep corn covered. Drain off liquid and rinse in cold water rubbing vigorously to remove hulls. Boil again to serve with gravy, fry in lard, pork fat, and bear grease or meat drippings. If allowed to dry, hominy will keep for 4 or 5 years with no special preparation or storing except to keep dry.

When the Corps descended the west side of the mountains, fish was a main supply of food for the Indians. Most of the men did not care for it, so they survived on dog meat and some horsemeat. The Indians, after discovering how to make portable soup, figured out a way to make fish soup.

FISH SOUP

1 large cube of portable soup
2 handfuls of fresh or dried fish
2 cups water
Watercress, Sweet grasses cut up
Any available spices

Bring to a boil in a kettle and serve with seeds or nuts on top

---

When the Corps descended the mountains and started to eat fish, with the Nez Perce, it took it's toll. Lewis and Clark anticipated this and carried certain medicines with them. 1. Peruvian bark. 2. Assafoetic. 3. Colombo. 4. Magnesia. 5. Wintergreen/ Peppermint. 6. Copaiboe. 7. Flower or Sulfur.

Most of the medicines that Lewis carried are what we refer as spices today.

November 13th, 1805. First Corps members to see the Pacific Ocean were Private John Colter, Private Alexander Willard and Private George Shannon. The Mountain man story of "Colter's Run is the most famous story of the

Expedition. John Colter received an early discharge and return to the mountains to trap with Manuel Lisa, a well-known trapper and trader with the Indians. Colter was captured and told if he could out run the Indians he would be free. It was on this run that he discovered the area known as "Colters Hell". Today we know it as the first National Park, "Yellowstone".

Seven of the men returned to the Rockies to live and work and trap. They lived short lives and were killed by the Indians.

Wisdom MT. was named for a virtue of Pres. Jefferson for having the courage and wisdom to launch the Corps of discovery.

The Corps tasted for the 1st time on *November 4, 1805* the root called Wapato. It is an under water starchy root that they dried and fixed in various ways. It could be ground into flour or used in soups and cooked with meat. It was used by the lower Columbia Indians.

WAPITI

The Elk as it is nick named, was one of the principle staples in their diet. The expedition left Camp Wood on May 14, 1804. About a month later, on June 17^{th,} when they had reached Carol County, Missouri, Lewis described the country as abounding in Elk, Bear and deer. Clark mentioned sighting Elk on July 12th, and 2 days later Patrick Gass mentioned sighting Elk in his journals by could not kill any. They killed the 1st Elk on August 1st, 1804. One Elk they killed stood over 5 feet high and weighed about 600 lbs. The expedition hunters killed at least 117 elk in Montana, and 40% of them East of the Mountains. The uses of Elk hides are mentioned often. *FEBRUARY 26th, 1806 the men have provided them selves verry amply with mockersons and leather clothing. Meriwether Lewis. Ft Clatsop. Patrick Gass reported they made 338 pairs of Mockersons. Most made of Elk skins.*

Kamass root or Wild Hyacinth (Also called Camas)

This root is shaped like an onion and is small like a hickory nut. It bears a pretty blue flower and grows on rocky hills. The root is harvested in June and July. When eaten raw, the taste is quite pleasant. When boiled, it sometimes resembles the common potato. The Indian mode for preparing it was described by Joseph Whitehouse in his journals on September 22, 1805 as they descended the Lolo Trail on to the prairie near today's, Grangeville, Idaho. " the Indians gave us such food as they had to eat, consisting of roots of different kinds which was sweet and good. also red and black haws and c. the roots which they made use of for food is plenty, this prairies are covred with them. They are much like potatoes when they are cooked, and they have a curious way of cooking them. Thy have places made in the form of a small coal pit, and they heat stone in the pit, then water to raise a steem, then put on large loves of the pounded potatoes and 8 or 10 bushels of the potatoes on at once then cover them with wet straw and earth. in that they sweet them untill they are cooked, and when they take them out they pound some of them up fine and make them into loaves and cakes. They dry the cakes ad string them on strings, in such a way that they would keep a year and handy to carry, any journey". Joseph Whitehouse.

JANUARY 26, 1806

I purchased a little of the berry bread and a few of their roots for which I gave small fish hooks which they appeared fond of.

The natives either eat these berrys when ripe or immediantly from the bushes or dryed in the sun or by means of their swating kilns: very very frequently they pound them and bake them in large loaves of 10 or 15 pounds: this bread keeps very well during one season and retains the moist juices of the fruit much better than by any other method of preservation. This bread is broken and stired in cold water until it be sufficiently thick and then eaten, in this way the natives most generally use it.

Meriwether Lewis

While living at Fort Mandan for the winter of 1804-1805 the Corps worked very hard to prepare for the next portion of their trip. Each man who traveled with them had a specific purpose. While Lewis and Clark were at Camp Wood from August 1803 to May 14,1804 they interviewed lots of men who wanted to apply for the expedition. Lists have been found that Clark made with checks and comments by some of the names while deciding who was to accompany the Captains on the trek west.

Sergeants

Patrick Gass was promoted to Sergeant when Floyd died. He was the Corps last survivor. He wrote a journal of the entire trip.

John Ordway returned to Washington with Lewis and Chief Sheheke. He was born in New Hampshire but returned to Missouri where he died in 1817.

Nathaniel Pryor retired from the Army in 1810. Re-enlisted in 1813 and fought in the Battle of New Orleans with Andrew Jackson. He married an Osage woman and traded on the Arkansas River then returning to Montana. The Pryor Mountains are named after him as well as Pryor, Montana and Oklahoma.

PRIVATES

William Bratton died in 1841.
John Collins died in 1823
John Colter died in 1813.
Pierre Cruzatte thought to be dead by 1825.
Joseph Field died in 1807.
Rubin Field died in Kentucky 1823.
Robert Frazer died in 1837.
George Gibson died in 1809.
Silas Goodrich stayed in the Army after the expedition.
Hugh Hall last seen in St. Lewis in 1809 when Lewis lent him money.
Thomas Howard. Francois Labiche settled in St. Louis area.
Hugh McNeal dead by 1828.
John Newman killed by the Yankton Sioux in 1838.
John Potts killed in the Three Forks area in 1808.
George Shannon died in 1836.
John Shields died in 1809.
Peter M. Weiser killed by Blackfoot Indians in 1808 by Three Forks, Montana.
William Werner thought to be in Virginia.
Joseph Whitehouse deserted from the Army in 1817.
Alexander Hamilton Willard died in 1865.
Richard Windsor unknown.

Letter from President Thomas Jefferson

Transcribed and Edited by Gerard W. Gawalt,

To <Captain> Meriwether Lewis esq. Capt. of the 1st. regimt, of Infantry of the US. of A.

Your situation as Secretary of the President of the US. has made you acquainted with the objects of my confidential message of Jan. 18. 1803 to the legislature; you have seen the act they passed, which they expressed in general terms, was meant to sanction these objects, and you are appointed to carry them into execution.

Instruments for ascertaining by celestial observations, the geography of the country through which you will pass, have been already provided. Light articles for barter and presents among the Indians, arms for your attendants, say from 10. to 12. men, boats, tents, & other travelling apparatus with ammunition, medicine, surgical instruments and provisions you will have prepared with such aids as the Secretary at War can yield in his department; & from him also you will recieve authority to engage among our troops, by voluntary agreement, the number of attendants above mentioned, over whom you, as their commanding officer, are invested with all the powers the laws give in such a case.

As your movements while within the limits of the US. will be better directed by occasional communications, adapted to circumstances as they arise, they will not be noticed here. What follows will respect your proceedings after your departure from the United States.

Your mission has been communicated to the ministers here from France, Spain & Great Britain, and through them to their governments; & such assurances given them as to it's objects as we trust will satisfy them. The country <of Lousiana> having been ceded by Spain to France, <and possession by this time probably given,> the passport you have from the minister of France, the representative of the present sovereign of the country, will be a protection <against> with all its subjects, & that from the minister of England will entitle you to the friendly aid of any traders of that allegiance with whom you may happen to meet.

The object of your mission is to explore the Missouri river, & such principal stream of it as by it's course and communication with the waters of the Pacific ocean whether the Columbia, Oregon, Colorado or any other river may offer the most direct & practicable water communication across this continent for the purposes of commerce.

Beginning at the mouth of the Missouri, you will take <careful> observations of latitude & longitude at all remarkable points on the river, & especially at the mouth of rivers, at rapids, at islands, & other places & objects distinguished by such <durable> natural marks & characters of a durable <nature> kind as that they may with certainty be recognized hereafter. The course of the river between these points of observation ma be supplied by the compass, the log-line & by time, corrected by the observations themselves. The variations of the compass too, in different places should be noticed.

The interesting points of the portage between the heads of the Missouri, & of the water offering the best communication with the Pacific ocean, should also be fixed by observation, & the course of that water to the ocean, in the same manner as that of the Missouri.

Your observations are to be taken with great pains & accuracy, to be entered distinctly & intelligibly for others, as well as yourself, to comprehend all the elements necessary, with the aid of the usual tables, to fix the latitude and longitude of the places at which they were taken, and are to be rendered to the war office for the purpose of having the calculations made concurrently by proper persons within the US. several copies of these as well as of your other notes should be made at leisure times, & put into the care of the most trust-worthy of your attendants, to guard by multiplying them against the accidental losses to which they will be exposed. A further guard would be that one these copies be on the paper of the birch, as less liable to injury from damp than common paper.

The commerce which may be carried on with the people inhabiting the line your will pursue, renders a knolege of those people important. You will therefore endeavour to make yourself acquainted <with> as far as a diligent pursuit of your journey shall admit, with the names of the nations & their numbers;

the extent & limits of their possessions;

their relations with other tribes of nations;

their language, traditions, monuments;

their ordinary occupations in agriculture, fishing, hunting, war, arts & the implements for these;

their food, clothing, & domestic accomodations;

the diseases prevalent among them, & the remedies they use;

moral & physical circumstances which distinguish them from the tribes we know;

peculiarities in their laws, customs & dispositions;

and articles of commerce they may need or furnish & to what extent.

And considering the interest which every nation has in extending & strengthening the authority of reason & justice among the people around them, it will be useful to acquire what knolege you can of the state of morality, religion, & information among them; as it may better enable those who may endeavor to civilize & instruct them, to adapt their measures to the existing notions & practices of those on whom they are to operate.

Other objects worthy of notice will be

the soil & face of the country it's growth & vegetable productions, especially those not of the US.

the animals of the country generally, & especially those not known in the US.

the remains & accounts of any which may be deemed rare or extinct;

the mineral productions of every kind; but more particularly metals; limestone, pit-coal, & salt-petre; salines & mineral waters, noting the temperature of the last & such circumstances as may indicate their character;

volcanic appearances;

climate, as characterized by the thermometer, by the proportion of rainy, cloudy, & clear days, by lightening, hail, snow, ice, by the access & recess of frost, by the winds prevailing at different seasons, the dates at which particular plants put forth or lose their flower, or leaf, times of appearance of particular birds, reptiles or insects.

Altho' your route will be along the channel of the Missouri, yet you will endeavor to inform yourself, by enquiry, of the character & extent of the country watered by it's branches & especially on it's Southern side, the North river or Rio Bravo which runs into the gulph of Mexico, and the North river, or Rio colorado which runs into the gulph of California, are understood to be the principal streams heading opposite to the waters of the Missouri, and running Southwardly. Whether the dividing grounds between the Missouri & them are mountains or flat lands, what are their distance from the Missouri, the character of the intermediate country, & the people inhabiting it, are worthy of particular enquiry. The Northern waters of the Missouri are less to be enquired after, because they have been ascertained to a considerable degree, & are still in a course of ascertainment by English traders, and travellers. But if you can learn any thing certain of the most Northern source of the Missisipi, & of it's position relatively to the lake of the woods, it will be interesting to us.

<Two copies of your notes at least & as many more as leisure will admit, should be made & confided to the care of the most trusty individuals of your attendants.> Some account too of the path of the Canadian traders from the Missisipi, at the mouth of the Ouisconsing to where it strikes the Missouri, & of the soil and rivers in its <traverses> course, is desirable.

In all your intercourse with the natives, treat them in the most friendly & conciliatory manner which their own conduct will admit; allay all jealousies as to the object of your journey, satisfy them of it's innocence, make them acquainted with the position, extent character, peaceable & commercial dispositions of the US. of our wish to be neighborly, friendly, & useful to them, & of our dispositions to a commercial intercourse with them; confer with them on the points most convenient as mutual emporiums, and the articles of most desireable interchange for them & us. If a few of their influential chiefs within practicable distance, wish to visit us, arrange such a visit with them, and furnish them with authority to call on our officers, on their entering the US. to have them conveyed to this place at the public expence. If any of them should wish to have some of their young people brought up with us, & taught such arts as may be useful to them, we will recieve, instruct & take care of them. Such a mission whether of influential chiefs or of young people would give some security to your own party.Carry with you some matter of the kinepox; inform those of them with whom you may be, of it's efficacy as a preservative from the smallpox; & instruct & encourage them in the use of it. This may be especially done wherever you winter.

As it is impossible for us to foresee in what manner you will be recieved by those people, whether with hospitality or hostility, so is it impossible to prescribe th exact degree of preserverance with which you are to pursue your journey. We value too much the lives of citizens to offer them to probable destruction. Your numbers will be sufficient to secure you against the unauthorised opposition of individuals or of small parties: but if a superior force authorised, or not authorised by a nation, should be arrayed against your further passage, and inflexibly determined to arrest it, you must decline it's farther pursuit, and return.In the loss of yourselves, we should lose also the information you will have acquired. By returning safely with that, you may enable us to renew the essay with better calculated means. To your own discretion therefore must be left the degree of danger you risk, and the point at which you should decline, only saying we wish you to err on the side of your safety, and to bring back your party safe even if it be with less information.

Pg 30

As far up the Missouri as the white settlements extend, an intercourse will probably be found to exist between them & the Spanish posts of St. Louis opposite Cahokia, or Ste. Genevieve opposite Kaskaskia. From still further up the river, the traders may furnish a conveyance for letters. Beyond that, you may perhaps be able to engage Indians to bring letters for the government to Cahokia or Kaskaskia, on promising that they shall there recieve such special compensation as you shall have stipulated with them. Avail yourself of these means to communicate to us, at seasonable intervals, a copy of your journal, notes & observations, of every kind, putting into cypher whatever might do injury if betrayed.

Should you reach the Pacific ocean inform yourself of the circumstances which may decide whether the furs of those parts may not be collected as advantageously at the head of the Missouri (convenient as is supposed to the waters of the Colorado & Oregan or Columbia) as at Nootka sound, or any other point of that coast; and that trade be consequently conducted through the Missouri & U.S. more beneficially than by the circumnavigation now practised.

On your arrival on that coast endeavor to learn if there by any port within your reach frequented by the sea-vessels of any nation, & to send two of your trusty people back by sea, in such way as <they shall judge> shall appear practicable, with a copy of your notes: and should you be of opinion that the return of your party by the way they went will be eminently dangerous, then ship the whole, & return by sea, by the way either of cape Horn, or the cape of good Hope, as you shall be able. As you will be without money, clothes or provisions, you must endeavor to use the credit of the U.S. to obtain them, for which purpose open letters of credit shall be furnished you, authorising you to draw upon the Executive of the U.S. or any of it's officers, in any part of the world, on which draughts can be disposed of, & to apply with our recommendations to the Consuls, agents, merchants, or citizens of any nation with which we have intercourse, assuring them, in our name, that any aids they may furnish you, shall be honorably repaid, and on demand. Our consuls Thomas Hewes at Batavia in Java, Wm. Buchanan in the Isles of France & Bourbon & John Elmslie at the Cape of good Hope will be able to supply your necessities by draughts on us.

Should you find it safe to return by the way you go, after sending two of your party round by sea, or with your whole party, if no conveyance by sea can be found, do so; making such observations on your return, as may serve to supply, correct or confirm those made on your outward journey.

On re-entering the U.S. and reaching a place of safety, discharge any of your attendants who may desire & deserve it, procuring for them immediate paiment of all arrears of pay & cloathing which may have incurred since their departure, and assure them that they shall be recommended to the liberality of the legislature for the grant of a souldier's portion of land each, as proposed in my message to Congress; & repair yourself with your papers to the seat of government <to which I have only to add my sincere prayer for your safe return>.

To provide, on the accident of your death, against anarchy, dispersion, & the consequent danger to your party, and total failure of the enterprize, you are hereby authorized, by any instrument signed & written in your own hand, to name the person among them who shall succeed to the command on your decease, and by like instruments to change the nomination from time to time as further experience of the characters accompanying you shall point out superior fitness: and all the powers and authorities given to yourself are, in the event of your death, transferred to, & vested in the successor so named, with further power to him, and his successors in like manner to name each his successor, who, on the death of his predecessor, shall be invested with all the powers & authorities given to yourself.

Given under my hand at the city of Washington this 20th day of June 1803.* ... Th. J. Pr. U.S. of A.

MS in the hand of Thomas Jefferson. Thomas Jefferson Papers, Library of Congress.

*Dateline and signature were written on a later date and with a different pen and ink, than the body of the document, which had been sent to Lewis, James Madison, Levi Lincoln, and Albert Gallatin for their comments in April.

SOME SUGGESTED BOOKS TO ENJOY

1. Undaunted Courage *by Steven Ambrose.*
2. The Lewis & Clark Journals *by Dr Gary Moulton.*
3. Traveling the Lewis and Clark Trail *by Julie Farnslow.*
4. The Incredible Journey of Lewis and Clark *by Rhoda Blumberg.*
5. Along the Trail with Lewis and Clark *by Barbara Firer-Vicky Soderberg.*
6. Lewis and Clark *by Scholastic from George Sullivan.*
7. The Journals of Lewis and Clark *edited by Bernard DeVoto*
8. The Journals of Patrick Gass *by Carol Lynn MacGregor.*
9. The Men of the Lewis and Clark Expedition *by Charles G. Clarke*
10. Lewis and Clark among the Indians *by James P. Rhonda*
11. The Truth about Sacajawea *by Kenneth Thomasma*
12. The Real Thomas Jefferson *by Andrew M. Allison.*
13. Colter's Run *by Judith Edwards*

There are so many great books to read! I hope you will take time to enjoy them with your kids or grandkids.

♦ Imagine the joy that President Jefferson felt when James Neely delivered a letter on October 26th, 1806 from Lewis. It took over a month to get the letter from St. Louis to Washington DC. Unfortunately, no record, of what happened when Jefferson and Lewis met ,was ever recorded. One can only imagine the feelings they felt.

Main Meal Dishes

How we Cook it Today!

Bean Dishes

Your Oven

or

Dutch oven

Now

Roasts & Casseroles

WENDY'S BLACK POT DEER ROAST

Try this one
you'll love it

1 can mushroom soup
1 can crushed tomatoes
1 pkg. dry onion soup mix
Salt and pepper to taste
1/4 cup Cider vinegar
3 to 4 pound roast (use beef, pork, elk, or moose)
2 small cans green chilies

Mix first five ingredients together in a 10-inch warmed and oiled Dutch oven. Add roast and spoon mixture over it. Roast will be almost covered. Top with chilies. Cover and bake in your oven on 300 degrees for 3 or 4 hours. In your Collapsible Volcano, place 12 briquettes in a circle underneath on bottom grill. In 2 hrs, replace briquettes, and for coals only, replace coals every 30 to 40 minutes.

BAKED BLACK POT DUCK

Thoroughly check over fillets to remove all stray shot.
Marinate duck (or goose or crane) fillets for 2 hours in enough water to cover bird with 1/2 cup of cider vinegar, lightly peppered and salted (if desired).
Pierce the meat with a fork to allow water to penetrate into meat.
Remove from water, and place in a warmed and oiled 12" Dutch oven.
Add 1/4 cup cooking oil, 1/2 cup Water, 1/2 cup chopped celery, 1 medium onion sliced and 2 chicken bouillon cubes.
Sprinkle with an All Purpose Seasoning,
Cooking time will vary with the thickness of the cut of meat.
Waiting for the smell is the best way to tell when it is done.
Cook low and slow for 2 hrs at 300 degrees or lower, for an extremely tender bird.

Turkey and Chicken can be done the same way.
Use 10 coals on a 12" Dutch oven.
For coals only, 10 bottom and 13 on top.

Turkey Stir-Fry

Cut 2-pound turkey breast into 1/2-inch strips.
1/4 cup oil
1/4 cup soy sauce (low sodium)
1 tbsp. horseradish
1 tsp. garlic powder
1/3 cup oil
Stir-fry vegetable mix
1 tsp. minced garlic
10 oz. can chicken broth
Black pepper, to taste
1/2 to 1 cup slivered almonds
1/4 cup white wine or 7-up (or Sprite)
3 tbsp. soy sauce
3 tbsp. cornstarch

Marinate turkey in 2 cans 7-up for 2 hours. Preheat Dutch oven with 1/3 cup oil. Remove turkey from marinade and cook in hot oil till meat changes color. Add: prepared stir-fry mix (or make your own). Cover and simmer until vegetables are tender and add remaining ingredients. Cook for and additional 4 minutes, stirring constantly. Serve with rice.

Yaller Bread with Pintos

Cornbread, also known as corn pone, johnnycake, and yaller bread, was always more common than sourdough down in South Texas. Cowboys there had to eat their yaller bread with molasses and frijoles. This one already has the frijoles in it.

This recipe is courtesy of
Bobby Taylor

1 1/2 cups buttermilk
3 eggs lightly beaten
3 tbsp. sugar
1 tsp. baking soda
1/2 cup Ranch Beans
1/2 cup fresh corn kernels
1 cup flour
1 1/2 cups fine yellow cornmeal
1/2 cup butter. Melted

Preheat the oven to 375 degrees. Prepare a 9 or 10-inch cast-iron skillet by rubbing with oil or melted butter and set aside. Combine the buttermilk, eggs, sugar and melted butter and mix well. Add the beans and the corn. Sift together the flour and cornmeal. Slowly add the flour mixture to the liquids, whisking until well incorporated. Whisk in the melted butter and pour the batter into pan or cast iron skillet and bake for 40 minutes covered, or until a toothpick comes out clean.

RANCH BEANS

People like their beans without a lot of frills in West Texas. Serve these with Cow Town Coleslaw and Yaller Bread with Pintos for a COWBOY version of a health food lunch.

4 cups dried pinto beans
4 cups minced yellow onions (1/2 cups diced)
1/2 cup pure chili powder
1/4 cup kosher salt
1/2 bunch cilantro, stemmed and chopped
4 tbsp. oil
2 cups diced red bell pepper
2 cups diced green bell pepper

Wash the beans and sort through them to remove any foreign particles and broken beans. In a stockpot, cover the beans with cold water by 6 inches and soak them 6 hours, or overnight. Be sure the beans remain covered with water during the soaking process. Drain the beans and return them to the same pan. Cover them with fresh water by 1/2 inch.

Add the minced onions, chili powder salt and cilantro and stir to blend. Bring the beans to a boil over medium heat. Add 1/2 cup Cider vinegar to help the tenderizing process. Reduce heat, cover and cook until the beans are tender about 2 1/2 hours. From time to time check and stir the beans. If necessary add water as needed. Near the end of the cooking time the liquid should be almost absorbed. Close to serving time, heat the olive oil in a large sauté' pan. When the oil is very hot, add the diced onion and peppers and cook them quickly about 6 minutes, stirring and tossing, until crisp but tender. Stir this mixture into the beans. Serve at once. Serves 10

This recipe is courtesy of
Bobby Taylor

FRY PAN OR SKILLET MEALS

ELK HOT DISH

1 lb. Elk steak, cubed (beef, pork or veal can be substituted)
3 tbsp. butter
3 med. onions, sliced
1 1/2 cup diced celery
1/2 cup rice
1 sm. can of mushrooms
1/4 green pepper, diced
3 tbsp. soy sauce
1 can mushroom soup
1 can chicken-rice soup
1/2 tsp. salt

Sauté meat in a 12 or 13 inch Fry pan with butter until brown. Set aside. Sauté onions in pan drippings until tender. Add meat and remaining ingredient except almonds, with 2 soup cans water; mix well. Simmer for 1 hour. Sprinkle with almonds. Simmer another 10 minutes and serve with Dutch oven rolls.

SKILLET SPAGHETTI

1 lb. Ground elk burger or hamburger
2 tbsp. oil
2 tsp. salt
3/4 cup chopped onions
1/3 cup chopped green pepper
1 clove garlic, minced (optional)
4 cups water
1/2 lb. spaghetti, broken into 2 inch pieces (about 2 1/2 cups)
1 can crushed tomatoes
1 medium jar of spaghetti sauce

In a large deep skillet, brown first six ingredients in shortening, and stir in water. Bring mixture to a boil; add sauce and tomatoes. Slowly simmer for 10 minutes, uncovered. Stir in broken up spaghetti or any pasta and simmer until the pasta is tender. For extra flavor, you can add 1/2 cup ketchup. Sprinkle with Parmesan cheese and serve with Garlic bread and green vegetable or salad.

LITTLE TWO-BIT CASSEROLE

In a 12 inch Dutch oven, Brown 1 lb. ground beef
Sauté 1/2 cup chopped onion and 1/2 cup green pepper.
Mix in 1 can vegetable soup and 1 can stewed tomatoes and 1/2
cup water. Add 1/2 tsp. salt, 1/2 tsp. pepper and 1 tbsp. sugar.
Add 2 or 3 cups of pasta and bake in your oven for 35 to 40
minutes. In your Collapsible Volcano, use 12 briquettes on the
bottom in a circle and wait for the smell. For briquettes only,
use 10 on the bottom and 15 on top. Before serving, sprinkle 1
cup of grated cheese on top and let melt.

- In all, the Corps killed 396 elk on their trip.

- 131 were killed at fort Clatsop for clothes and moccasins.

- The meat was dried for the return trip.

MEATY CALICO BEANS

1 lb. Hamburger
1 lb. sausage
4 slices bacon, chopped fine
1 can Baked Deans
1 can Kidney Beans
1/2 cup Catsup
1 tbsp. Vinegar
1/2 cup Onion, chopped fine
1 can Green Beans
1 can Waxed Beans, drained
1/2 cup Brown Sugar
1 tsp. Salt
1 tbsp. Worcestershire sauce

Cook hamburger, sausage, bacon and onion in a 12 inch Dutch
oven. Mix remaining ingredients and simmer for 20 to 25
minutes over 10 or 12 coals in your Collapsible Volcano. When
using briquettes only, 10 on bottom and 15 on top or bake at
350 degrees in your oven at home.

QUICK FRIENDSHIP MEAT PIE

2 cup diced cooked beef
1 can cream mushroom or celery soup
1 pkg. frozen mixed vegetables
1 onion, minced
1 tsp. Worcestershire sauce
Salt and Pepper to taste
2 pie pastry shells

Warm and oil a 12 inch Dutch oven. Place enough pastry shell in the oven to cover the bottom. Put all the ingredients in oven and cover with the soup. Put remaining pastry on top and brush with milk. Bake in your oven for 35 to 40 minutes. Use 9 briquettes on bottom and 15 on top in your Collapsible Volcano and 9 bottom and 15 top if using briquettes only.

Serve with Aunt Lizzies Beer Bread on page #88.
This will bring your friends back for seconds

LIMA'S AND SALT PORK

1/2 lb. dried lima beans
1/2 lb. salt pork, diced (or sub bacon)
1/2 tsp. Salt
1/2 cup cider vinegar
Water enough to cover beans
1 12-oz. can of kernel or fresh corn

Cover beans with water and vinegar, soak overnight; then drain. Place beans, pork, salt and enough water to cover, in a warmed and lightly oil 10 inch Dutch oven. Cook covered over low fire for 1 1/2 hours; add small amount of water if needed. Add corn; stir and cook for 15 minutes more.

MOUTH WATERING PORK ROAST WITH VEGETABLES

1-bag baby carrots
8-or-10 small red potatoes,
1/4 cup water plus 1 tbsp. cider vinegar.
1/2 tsp. dried rosemary
2 tbsp. cornstarch
1 tbsp. all purpose seasoning
Salt and pepper to taste
1 sliced medium onion

Warm and lightly oil a 12"-8 qt. deep Dutch oven. Place a 4 or 5 lb. Pork roast in the bottom. You can place the roast on a meat trivet to keep it out of the grease. Arrange onion slices around and on the roast. Sprinkle the spices on roast and place the vegetables around the roast. Pour the water and vinegar in the oven and place the lid on top. Bake the roast in your oven on 300 degrees for 2 to 2-1/2 hrs. When using the Collapsible Volcano, use 12 to 14 briquettes on the bottom in a circle. Using briquettes only, be sure to keep 10-to-12 on the bottom and 15 on the top. You will have to replace the briquettes 2-or-3 times to complete the cooking. To make gravy, pour pan juices into a glass measuring cup. If necessary, add water to make 1 cup. Add the cornstarch and stir until smooth stir into pan juices. Heat in bottom of Dutch to thicken. Season with salt and pepper.

HUNGRY BOY CASSEROLE

1 lb. hamburger
1/2 lb. sausage
1 cup chopped celery
1/2 cup chopped onion
1/2 cup chopped green pepper
3/4 cup roasted garlic sauce
1 clove garlic, minced
3/4 cup water
1 tsp. salt
1 tsp. paprika
1 can pork and beans
1 can peas or lima beans

Sauté in 10-inch Dutch oven, beef, celery, onion, green pepper and garlic, until vegetables are tender. Add remaining ingredients. Simmer for 30 to 45 minutes. Place biscuits on top of bean mixture and transfer the coals on top in your Collapsible Volcano. You can bake in your oven for 30 minutes on 350 degrees, or use coals only with 8 under and 11 on top.

this one is easy to get to taste great!

FOURTH OF JULY MEAT AND BEAN CASSEROLE

1/2 lb. sliced bacon, diced
1/2 lb. hamburger
1 large onion chopped
1 large can pork and beans
1 can lima beans cooked drained
1 can kidney beans, drained
1/2 cup Jack Daniels Barbecue sauce
1/2 cup ketchup
1/2 cup brown sugar, packed
1/2 tsp. Chili powder
2 tbsp. mustard
2 tbsp. molasses
1 tsp. Salt

In a 10-inch Dutch oven that has been warmed and oiled, cook bacon beef and onion. Add all remaining ingredients and bake in your oven at 350 degrees for about 45 minutes. In your Collapsible Volcano, place 10 or 12 briquettes on the bottom in a circle underneath and wait for the smell. With briquettes only, use 8 on the bottom and 11 on top. ENJOY

"We fired a Gun at sunrise in honour of the day, and continued our voyage; passed a creek on the North side and called it Pond creek, at one o' clock we stopped to dine. One of our people got snake bitten, but not dangerously. After dinner we continued our voyage, passed a creek on the north side which we called INDEPENDENCE, encampment on the north side at an old Indian village on a handsome prairie, and saluted the departing day with another gun."

July 4th 1804
-Patrick Gass-

ORANGE CUBE STEAK OR CHICKEN

12 steaks or boneless, skinless chicken breasts
6 slices ham
6 slices Swiss cheese or Monterey jack
1 orange
1 6 oz. box Stove Top Stuffing
1 small bottle orange marmalade
1/4 cup oil

Mix stuffing according to directions and add 1 tbs. orange rind and 1 tbs. orange juice. Flatten steaks or chicken breasts; lay 2, side by side. Place a thin layer of stuffing mix on 1 slice of steak or chicken. Lay 1 slice each ham and cheese across both pieces. Fold sandwich style, with steak or chicken on top and bottom. Repeat to make 6 bundles. You can tie with cord if you want. Melt oil in Dutch oven, place bundles in a pinwheel design. Spread orange marmalade thinly on top of each bundle. You can lay slices of onion and orange on top for decoration and to enhance the taste. Bake 350 degrees in your oven at home with the lid on. When using briquettes, place 12 coals under and 15 on top for 1 hr or until you can really smell it. Use 12 coals on the bottom in a circle with the Collapsible Volcano.

GARLIC SWISS STEAK

1/4 cup oil
7 to 10 cube steaks
1 onion chopped
2 stalks celery
2 cups sliced carrots
5 potatoes
1 can roasted garlic sauce
1 can tomato soup
1/4 cup flour

Flour both sides of the steak. In a 12-inch warmed and oiled Dutch oven, brown steaks in oil. Add chopped onions and celery. Stir in the rest of the ingredients and cook 1 hour. Use 12 coals on the top and 15 on bottom. Bake at 350 degrees in your oven at home, and in your Collapsible Volcano, 12 on the bottom in a circle.

♦ In the state of Washington, be sure to visit the Sacajawea State Park located 2 miles east of Pasco, WA. on US-12.

PORK CHOPS AND STUFFING

12 thinly sliced pork chops
1 onion, diced
4 celery stocks, diced
1 box sage stuffing
2 cans cream of mushroom soup
1 can cream of celery soup
1 can water

Prepare stuffing according to directions on package. Add celery and onions. Mix thoroughly. Place 1/3 cup dressing on a pork chop. Place another pork chop on top. Insert 2 or 3 toothpicks in chops to hold together. Place chops in 12-inch Dutch oven that has been warmed and oiled. You can brown on one side and turn over if you like. Pour the cream soups evenly over the top. Bake at 350 degrees for 1 hour. Use 12 coals on the bottom and 14 to 16 on top.

RODEO PORK WITH ONIONS

4 pork tenderloins cut in strips
3/4 tsp. pepper
1/4 tsp. crushed red chilies
6 medium onions, chopped
1-2 sweet red peppers cut into long strips
1/2 cup cooking oil
1 tsp. Paprika

In a 12 or 13-inch skillet, pour 1/4 cup oil and brown thin sliced strips or Pork. Add all other ingredients and remaining 1/4 cup of the oil. Sauté until blended well. Reduce heat. Cook over medium heat 15-20 minutes. Garnish with 1-inch cubes of Feta cheese, slices or onion and red peppers if desired.

- ♦ On November 4th, 1805 the Corps tasted the Wapato root for the first time.

- ♦ This root is still used by the lower Columbia Indians to make bread and soups.

SWEET AND SOUR PORK

In a small bowl, combine the following:
1/2 tsp. salt
1/4 tsp. Pepper
1/4 cup powdered sugar
Coat 3 cups of cubed pork. with the mixture:

Pour oil into wok. Add pork and stir-fry for about 10 minutes or until evenly browned and reduce heat. Add 1/4 cup water, Cover and simmer for 30 minutes or until pork is pork tender. Remove, cover and reduce heat. Push pork up the side. Add 2 tbsp. Butter. When butter is melted, add and stir-fry for 2 minutes. Add 1 cup finely chopped onion, 1 each 8 1/2-oz. can of diced bamboo shoots, drained.

Push mixture up on the side of the Wok. Add and cook 2 minutes:

1 pkg. frozen peas
3 tbsp. lemon juice
1/4 cup soy sauce.

Mix entire mixture together. Serve with rice or noodles.

BEEF AND BEAN SKILLET SUPPER

1/2 lb. lean tender beefsteak or hamburger
2 tbsp. oil
1 onion, chopped
2 cups French cut green beans (raw or frozen)
1 cup sliced celery
1 tbsp. cornstarch
1 tbsp. soy sauce
3/4 cup liquid, juice from mushrooms plus water
1 can mushrooms

Cut beef in strips and brown in oil. Add onions, beans and celery. Cook 4 to 6 minutes; stir. Combine cornstarch and soy sauce with liquid. Add to skillet with the mushrooms. Stir and simmer until liquid is shiny and beans are tender. Serve with hash browns, mashed or baked potatoes. Even rice works great.

♦ On November 15th thru the 25th, 1805 the Chinook Indians presented gifts of dried Salmon and Cranberries to the Corps.

1 can beef bouillon
4 to 5 lb. roast
6 potatoes
2 to 4 onions (chopped)
1 medium pkg. small carrots
10 sliced mushrooms
Add celery, green pepper and other vegetables as desired.

In a 12-inch Dutch oven, over 12 hot coals pour about 1/4 cup of vegetable oil and add beef bouillon over roast and place lid on oven. Bake 90 minutes and add all vegetables. Cook for another 30 to 45 minutes, depending on how crisp you like your vegetables. Waiting for the smell is the best way to tell when it is done. When cooking with coals only, use 10 on the bottom and 15 on top. Your Collapsible Volcano will take 12 in a circle on the bottom only. When using the Camp Chef 2 burner, be sure to use low heat with 12 coals on top.

Hint: To shorten cooking time, cube roast and pre-cook potatoes and carrots. This will shorten the time about an hour.

3-4 lb. roast
1 pkg. Dry beefy onion soup mix
1/2 cup Water
2 cans cream of mushroom soup
5 medium potatoes quartered
6 carrots sliced
1 cup Diced celery

Place the roast in a 12-inch Dutch oven that has been warmed and oiled. Place the roast in the oven on onion slices or a meat trivet if desired. Bake 1 hour on 12 coals in your stoves or on 10 bottom coals and 15 on top. Remove the lid and add potatoes, celery and carrots Put in remaining ingredients. Cook approximately 1 hour at 350 degrees. Keep the fire low on your propane stove.

◆ On October 16th thru 18th, 1805 the captains and crew met with the Yakima and Wanapam Indians. They received gifts of horse jerky and Fish.

OUT OF THE CHUTES BEEF GOULASH

1 1/2 lbs Stew beef
Flour, seasoned with salt and Pepper
3 tbsp. butter
1 medium onion, chopped
1 cup sliced celery
2 tsp. paprika
1 tsp. caraway seed
1 jar Roasted garlic Sauce
1/4 cup sour cream
3 cups cooked noodles

Roll beef cubes in seasoned flour and brown in butter. Sauté' onions, celery and paprika with beef cubes, caraway and Ragu' Italian cooking sauce and simmer covered for 1 hour. Dutch should be on 10 briquettes in your Collapsible Volcano. Blend in sour cream and heat thoroughly but do not allow sauce to boil. Serve over hot noodles or rice.

BEHIND THE CHUTES BEEF GOULASH

1 1/2 lbs. beef stew meat
1 cup chopped onion
2 cups water
2 tbsp. vinegar
1 tsp. paprika
1/2 tsp. caraway seeds
1 jar spaghetti sauce your choice
1 can tomato puree
1 small pkg. thin pasta noodles
1/2 tsp. Garlic salt
Salt and pepper to taste

Heat oil in 12-inch cast iron skillet over medium heat. Add beef and onion and Sauté, stirring occasionally until tender, about 5 minutes. Stir in water, spaghetti sauce, spices, vinegar, paprika and caraway seeds. Bring to boil. Reduce heat; cover and simmer for 1 1/4 hours. Stir in pasta and tomato puree. Cover and simmer about 30 minutes or until meat is tender.

SALMON SURPRISE

1 can salmon
1/2 cup cream of mushroom soup
1 1/2 cup soft bread crumbs
1/4 cup ketchup
2 eggs

Drain water off salmon and add water to make 1/2 cup. Mix the water with salmon and spoon into a warmed and oiled 10-inch Dutch Oven. Mix remaining ingredients together and pour over salmon. Bake at 350 degrees for 35 minutes in your oven at home. A piecrust can be placed in the bottom of the Dutch oven if you prefer. Use 10 to 12 coals on the bottom of your Collapsible Volcano, and 10 on bottom and 15 on top for briquettes only.

- On October 11th, 1805 the party stopped on their way to the Ocean with the "Alpowai" band of Nez Perz Indians.

- They purchased and traded for dogs, berries and dried fish.

CAMPERS STEW

2 lb. ground beef
1 onion
3 carrots
3 potatoes
Salt and pepper to taste
4 oz. can mushroom pieces
1 can cream of celery soup
3 stalks celery
1/2 cup water

Make 1-inch diameter meatballs with ground beef. Cut all vegetables into small bite sized pieces. Warm and oil a 12-inch shallow Dutch oven. Mix all ingredients and let stand 10 minutes. Bake with 10 coals bottom and 15 on top for 35 to 50 minutes. The smell will tell you when it is done. It will take 12 on the bottom in a circle for your Collapsible Volcano. Low heat on the bottom and 12 coals on top for your propane stove.

ORNERY OLE CUSS STEW

1 1/2 lbs ground meat
1/2 lb. ground hamburger
1/2 lb. sausage
2 cans whole chilies, rinsed
2 cups shredded cheddar and jack cheese
3/4 cup milk
1 egg
2 tbsp. Flour

Brown meat:
Make two layers of meat, chilies, and cheese
Mix egg, milk, and flour. Pour over the top of layers

Cook in 10 inch Dutch oven at 350 degrees for 30 minutes with 12 briquettes on top and 8 on the bottom. To double recipe increase time by 15 to 20 minutes.

♦ Private Reubin Fields and a Nez Perce man took a horse loaded with Kamas root and three large salmon to Lewis and the main party of the Corps.

CHUCK WAGON SKILLET SPAGHETTI

" This is a great Recipe"
Company

1 lb. hamburger
1/2 lb. sausage
6 slices bacon chopped
3 Onions chopped
1 tsp. Garlic salt
1 can tomato soup
3 bay leaves
1 cup sliced mushrooms
1 can chili sauce
1 tsp. Worcestershire sauce
1 1/2 cup grated cheese
2 cup broken spaghetti

In a warmed and oiled 12-inch skillet, place the first 5 ingredients and cook until brown. Add next 5 ingredients and simmer on low heat for 20 minutes. Then add rest of ingredients. Stir and then over top, sprinkle grated cheese and bake at 350 degrees for 30 minutes on a low heat. Serve with Garlic rolls baked in a 12-inch Dutch oven.

Hobo Surprise

1 lb. ground beef
1 egg
1 tsp. Salt and pepper to taste
1/2 cup Oatmeal, cracker crumbs, breadcrumbs or corn flakes
2/3 cup tomato juice
Onion, carrots, and potatoes

Mix ground beef, oatmeal, salt and pepper and tomato juice and egg. Warm and oil a 12-inch Dutch, in the bottom, place 6 or 7 hamburger patties. Salt and pepper to taste, and place potatoes, onions and carrots sliced thin on top of the meat mixture. Bake at 350 in your oven with the lid on, or 10 coals underneath in a circle and 15 on top. Wait for the smell to tell you when it's done. In your Collapsible Volcano, 12 coals underneath will cook it just fine.

> *"October 10th, 1805 This night we purchased and traded for dog and food and some dry fish from the Snake River Nez Perce! I could not eat the dog, but the others, including Lewis preferred it to horse*
>
> **William Clark**

Heavenly Hamburger Pies

1 onion, chopped
2 tbsp. vegetable oil
1 lb. Hamburger
1 tsp. salt
2 cans green chilies
1/4 tsp. oregano
1 can condensed tomato soup
1/2 cup Shredded Monterey Jack cheese

Heat a 12 or 13-inch skillet and cook onion in oil until wilted. Add beef, salt, chilies and oregano. Cook until lightly browned, breaking up meat with a fork. Add undiluted tomato soup and heat through. Reduce heat to low. Sprinkle with shredded cheese and cover with pie dough. Bake in oven at 350 degrees for 20 minutes or until golden brown. When using a Dutch oven, place 18 coals on top and 6 or 7 on top. Top coals are important to brown the crust.

Pie Dough

2 cups all purpose baking mix or Bisquick.
1/2 cup Milk
1 tbsp. Water

Mix for a piecrust

BUNK HOUSE ALL DAY STEW

2 lbs. cubed stew meat
6 medium Potatoes, cubed
6 medium Carrots, sliced
1 cup Celery slices
1 cup Onion, chopped
2 cans Condensed Tomato Soup
1/2 cup Water
1 pkg. Dried Onion Soup Mix
1 tsp. Thyme

In 10-inch Dutch oven or large skillet with lid, combine stew meat with Potatoes, carrots, celery, thyme, onions, soup, water, and dried onion soup mix; blend well. Cover and bake at 300 degrees 2 or 3 hours in your oven. In your Collapsible Volcano, place 12 briquettes in a circle in the bottom, or for briquettes only, 10 on the bottom and 15 on top. The smell will tell you when it is done.

BACK COUNTRY STEW

6 lbs. of elk, deer, moose, beef, pork, antelope or fowl
12 carrots sliced thin
8 large potatoes cubed
2 onions cubed
1 can beef or chicken broth
1 lb. whole fresh mushrooms
1 lb. frozen corn
2 cups minute rice
2 cans cream of celery soup
2 cans cream of mushroom soup
8 stocks of celery

Warm and oil a 12-inch deep Dutch oven. Put about 1/4 cup of oil in Dutch oven and brown meat, season to taste. Cut potatoes, carrots, celery and onions into bite size pieces and add to meat. Add 1 can of cream of chicken soup, 1 can of cream of mushroom soup, rice, corn and mushrooms. Add the other 2 cans of soup and enough water to fill the Dutch oven. Cook over constant heat approximately 1 1/2 hours. Use 10 coals bottom and 13 to 14 on top. Bake at 350 degrees in your oven at home. The smell will tell you when it is done. Baking powder biscuits can be cooked on top.

SWEET AND SOUR MEAT BALLS

1 lb., Elk, venison of any kind, beef, pork or combination of
1 egg
1/2 cup breadcrumbs, corn flakes or oatmeal
1/2 cup ketchup
1 small onion
1 tsp. salt
1/4 tsp. pepper
4 tbsp. brown sugar

Sauce:

2 beef bouillon cubes
1 cup boiling water
1 tbsp. cornstarch

In a 10-inch Dutch oven that has been warmed place 1/4 cup oil. Mix the first 8 ingredients to make a meat-loaf mixture. Brown the meatballs in the oven. Bring water to a boil and dissolve bouillon cubes. Pour over the Browned meatballs. Bake at 350 in your oven, and over 12 coals in a circle underneath the oven in the Collapsible Volcano. Using coals only, 10 on the bottom and 15 on top. Serve over rice.

This would have made the Indians real Happy

STEW DO IN A SKILLET

1 1/2 lb., hamburger, browned
2 cup potatoes, cubed, cooked
2 cup mixed vegetables
1 cup frozen green beans

Blend all and add water until almost covered in skillet. Simmer until thick & vegetables are done. Serve with grated cheese. This mix can also be made into meat pie by placing crust over the top.

Lewis carried alot of today's spices for Medicinal Purposes (Ginger, alum, cinnamon, allspice etc.

ROAST BEEF AND BEANS

1 pound dry pinto beans
1 each 6 pound beef rump roast
1 tbsp. lard or shortening
1 cup green pepper strips
2 medium onions sliced
2 cups V-8 juice
1/2 cup Ketchup
1/2 cup water
2 tbsp. cider vinegar
2 tbsp. brown sugar
2 tbsp. salt
1 tsp. each dry mustard and thyme

Wash beans; cover with cold water and let soak overnight. Bring beans to a boil and cook 1 hour; drain, discarding water. Place the roast in warm oil in a large Dutch oven, 12-inch deep. Add peppers and onions and cook until tender. Add beans and remaining ingredients. Cover and bake in a 350-degree oven for 2 1/2 to 3 hours or until beans are tender and meat is done. When using the Collapsible Volcano, place 12 coals in a circle underneath in the stove. For coals only, use 10 on the bottom and 15 on top. The smell will tell you when it is done.

ITALIAN BROCCOLI AND CHICKEN SUPREME

Use a 12" Dutch oven.

10 Chicken breast halves
2 cans Creamed Corn
1 can Water
3/4 cup white Wine
2 cup Broccoli
Salt/pepper to taste
1 tsp. Oregano
1 tsp. Garlic salt
1 Onion
1 Red bell pepper
2 small cans mushrooms drained
2 cubes Butter

Chunk chicken to bite-sized pieces and brown in butter. Dump in creamed corn, can of water, and wine. Stir; add salt, pepper and all spices. Add sliced onion, mushrooms, and bite-sized broccoli. Add course diced red bell peppers and let simmer 20 minutes to combine flavors. Ladle over a bed of rice or pasta. Place over 10 briquettes in your Collapsible Volcano, or 10 on the bottom and 12 on the top for briquettes only. Low flame for propane stove.

RED SAUCE PORK CHOPS

6 pork chops
1/2 cup flour
1 tsp. salt
2 tbsp. shortening
1 can whole cranberry sauce
1 cup water
2 cups sugar

Roll chops in flour and salt. Brown chops on both sides, in shortening, using the bottom of a 12-inch Dutch oven. Put chops in single layer in oven. Combine water and sugar; pour over all and cover pan. Bake chops at 350 degrees for 50 minutes or until you can smell it. Place 12 coals in the bottom of your stove in a circle and 10 under and 15 on top for briquettes only. Listen to you oven, it will tell you when its done.

If you like the you'll love this one.

If you don't like cranberries try Blueberries grape or orange jam.

ENCHILADAS DUTCH OVEN STYLE

1 doz. corn tortillas
2 cans enchilada sauce
3 cans tomato soup
2 lbs. White and yellow grated cheese
2 large onions diced
2 lbs. Hamburger
1/2 lb. sausage

Warm and oil a 12-inch Dutch oven. Cook meats in Dutch oven and drain off grease. Remove meat from oven. Mix soup and enchilada sauce. Put a little of the sauce mixture in bottom of a Dutch oven.

Dip tortilla in sauce mixture on both sides. Put in meat, onion and cheese: Roll up and lay in pan. Pour excess sauce over enchiladas and add grated cheese. Bake at 350 degrees for 1 hour or until done. Place 12 lit coals in a circle in the bottom of your Collapsible Volcano, or 10 on the bottom and 15 on top when using briquettes only. The smell will tell you when it is done.

Easy easy easy & Good

STEAK STYLE MEAT LOAF

2 lbs. ground beef
1 onion chopped fine
1 cup bread crumbs
2 eggs
1 tbsp. steak sauce
1 can vegetable soup

Mix well and season to taste. Put in a 10 - Dutch oven. Bake for 1 1/2 hrs at 350 degrees. Crackers or Oatmeal can replace breadcrumbs

*Sept 20, 1805
  After climbing up and down the Bitter Root Mountains in snow, (their only source of water), and being as wet and as cold in every part as I ever was in my life. Captain Clark led an advance party of hunters down to Weippe Prairie which was beautiful and at long last level. Nez Perce were collecting Camas roots. These they shared with the Corps along with berries, Fish and some bison.

Meriwether Lewis

CHIMICHANGAS

1 lb. Hamburger
1 medium onion, chopped
1 clove garlic, minced
1 can tomato Soup
1 can chopped green chilies, drained
1 tbsp. vinegar
1 tsp. All purpose Seasoning
1/2 tsp. ground cumin
10 or 12 flour tortillas (8-inch)
1 cup shredded Cheese Shredded lettuce

In 10-inch skillet over medium heat, cook ground beef, onion and garlic until browned, stirring occasionally to break up meat. Pour off fat. Stir in Soup, chilies, vinegar, Seasoning and cumin; reduce heat. Simmer 10 to 15 minutes or until most of the liquid evaporates. Remove from heat and cool slightly. Spoon 1/4 cup filling down center of one tortilla. Top with 2 tbsp. Cheese. Fold in sides of tortilla and roll up tortilla around filling. Secure with a toothpick. Assemble 2 or 3 at a time. In 12-inch skillet, heat 1 inch oil to 350 degrees. Fry chimichangas 2 minutes or until golden, turning once. Remove and drain on paper towels.
Garnish with lettuce and Toppings.

There are many versions of this Southern recipe. Most include chicken, pork, sausage, shrimp, rice, and spices, in addition to other ingredients.

1 cup cut up chicken
2 tbsp. vegetable oil
3/4 cup diced smoked ham
1 smoked sausage, sliced 1/2 inch thick
1 lb. boneless pork loin, cubed
1 1/2 cups chopped onion
1 cup chopped celery
1 large green pepper, chopped
2 cloves garlic, minced
1/4 tsp. hot pepper sauce
2 bay leaves
1 1/2 tsp. Salt
1 1/2 tsp. Dried oregano
1/4 tsp. white pepper
1/2 tsp. black pepper
1 tsp. thyme
4 medium tomatoes, peeled and chopped
1 8-oz. can tomato sauce
1 14 1/2-oz. can chicken broth
1/2 cup chopped green onion
2 cups rice, uncooked

my Grandma did this one style ... She's from Mississippi

In large 12-inch Dutch oven, heat oil over medium heat.
Stir in ham, sausage, and pork and chicken.
Sauté until lightly browned, stirring frequently, 4-8 minutes.
Stir in onion, celery; and green pepper; sauté until crisp-tender, about 5 minutes.
Stir in garlic, hot pepper sauce, bay leaves, salt, oregano, white pepper, black pepper, and thyme.
Cook over medium heat for 5 minutes, stirring constantly and scraping pan bottom.
Stir in tomatoes and cook 5-8 minutes, stirring occasionally.
Stir in tomato sauce and chicken broth and bring to a boil.
Stir in green onion and rice.
Bake covered at 350 for 20-25 minutes or until rice is tender.
Remove bay leaves and serve immediately.

May 13th, 1805
"The party killed several deer and some elk. Principally for the benefit of their skins, which are necessary to them for clothing."
Meriwether Lewis

TAMALE CASSEROLE

3 cups corn chips
1 can tamales
1 cup chopped onion
1 can chili
1 cup grated Cheddar cheese

Warm and oil a 10-inch Dutch oven. Place 2 cups of the corn chips in the bottom of the oven. Arrange tamales on top of the chips and cover with the chopped onion. Pour the can of chili over all and top with the remaining cup of corn chips and the grated cheese. Bake 350 for 25 minutes. Put 8 coals on the bottom and 14 on top. Using your Collapsible Volcano, 12 on the bottom in a circle.

BEAN DIP CHILI

1 1/2 lbs. ground beef
1 can (1 lb.) tomatoes
1/2 cup water
1 envelope chili seasoning mix
1 large can refried beans

Brown the beef and stir in remaining ingredients. Simmer five to ten minutes. (Be sure to remove excess fat after the meat has browned before adding the other ingredients.) Bean Dip Chili can also be used as a hot dip. Serve it with corn chips.

GLAZED HAM STEAK

1 or 2 Ham steaks 1 inch thick
1 can (12 oz.) Apricot nectar
2 tsp. Worcestershire Sauce
2 tsp. Brown Sugar

Score fat edges of ham steaks. Place in a warmed and oiled 12-inch Dutch oven. Combine remaining ingredients and pour mixture over ham. Bake 35 minutes at 300 degrees in your oven. Using coals, place 10 on the bottom and 12 on top. Just 10 in your stove for a lower temperature!

June 21st, 1805
"Great falls of the Missouri several men employed in haeving and graneing elk hides for the iron boat, as it is called.

William Clark

♦ Lewis designed an iron boat, in pieces, which they carried up the Missouri river to the great falls area. After trying in vain to assemble it, they decided it wouldn't work.

No-Fuss Chicken

1 bottle (16 ounces) Russian or Catalina salad dressing
2/3 cup apricot preserves
2 envelopes dry onion soup mix
16 boneless skinless chicken breast halves

In a bowl, combine dressing, preserves and soup mix. Place chicken in a warmed and oiled 12-inch Dutch oven. Top with dressing mixture. Cover and bake at 350 degrees for 45 to 50 minutes Bake, until chicken juices run clear or you can smell it. In your Collapsible Volcano, 12 coals on the bottom in a circle. When using coals only, place 10 on the bottom and 15 on top.

February 19th, 1806 - (Fort Clatsop)
"Sergeant Gass returned with the flesh of 8 elk and 7 skins. We had the skins divided among the messes in order that they might be prepared for covering our baggage when we set out in the spring".

Meriwether Lewis

Sweet and Sour Pork Kabobs

1 medium size bag baby carrots
1 medium size can chunked pineapple
1/4 cup red wine vinegar
1 tbsp. cooking oil
1 tbsp. soy sauce
1 1/2 tsp. cornstarch
1 tsp. sugar
1 clove garlic, minced
12 ounces lean boneless pork, cut into 1-inch pieces
1 small green pepper, cut into 1-inch squares
1 small sweet red pepper, cut into 1-inch squares

In a saucepan, cook carrots until tender and drain well. Drain pineapple, saving the juice. For sauce, in a saucepan combine reserved pineapple juice, vinegar, oil, soy sauce, cornstarch, sugar, and garlic. Cook and stir till thickened and bubbly. Thread cooked carrots, pineapple, green and red pepper, and pork on skewers, leaving 1/4 inch between each piece of food. Grill kabobs on an uncovered grill directly over medium-hot coals for 8 to 12 minutes turning often or till pork is no longer pink. Brush often with sauce.

Grab 2 few mushroom's tp,

LAMB AND RICE SKILLET DINNER

3 lbs lamb stew meat
1/4 cup oil
1 cup rice
1 1/2 cups boiling water
1 jar Ragu' Italian Cooking Sauce
1 tsp. grated lemon rind
1 package (10 oz) frozen Italian Style Vegetables
1/4 cup water

Brown lamb slices in oil in large skillet. Add rice and brown lightly. Add boiling water, Ragu' Italian Cooking Sauce and lemon rind. Bring to a boil, cover and simmer 40 minutes Add vegetables and 'A cup water. Stir and cook 10 minutes.

LAMB WITH ZUCCHINI AND MACARONI

4 cups zucchini, sliced
1/2 cup each chopped celery and chopped onion
1/4 cup olive oil
1 lb ground lamb
3 cups cooked elbow macaroni
(1 1/2 cups uncooked)
1 jar Ragu' Italian Cooking Sauce
1 tsp. salt
1/4 tsp. pepper
1 tsp. oregano
4 oz. mozzarella cheese, sliced

Warm and oil a 12-inch oven. Brown the lamb, and add zucchini, celery and onion to the meat mix cook until tender. Mix macaroni, Ragu' Italian Cooking Sauce and seasonings in with zucchini. Sprinkle cheese on top and bake for 30 minutes. Use 12 coals in your Collapsible Volcano and when using coals only, 10 bottom and 15 top.

LAMB & EGGPLANT STEW

1 tbsp. oil
2 lbs lean lamb, cubed
1 large eggplant, unpeeled, cubed (6 cups)
1 clove garlic, minced
1 large onion, chopped
1 jar Roasted Garlic sauce
1 cup water
2 tsp salt
1/4 tsp. pepper
1 bay leaf
1/2 tsp. thyme
2 tbsp. parsley flakes
Dehydrated mint optional
Leaves for garnish

Brown meat thoroughly in a large cast iron, 13-inch skillet in oil. Add all remaining ingredients, except mint. Bring to a boil, cover and simmer 1-1/2 to 2 hours, stirring frequently. Sprinkle mint leaves on top just before serving. Serve over buttered rice.

"Great Taste"
Good Food
Share it with
Company"

CIVILIANS

Charbonneau, Toussaint - About 47 years old in 1805, he was the oldest person on the expedition. A French Canadian trader, he had lived among the Hidatsa Indians for several years before the Corps hired him as an interpreter.

Charbonneau, Jean Baptiste - Born February 11th, 1805. He was three months old when the Corps left Fort Mandan. He traveled the entire trip on a cradleboard on his mothers back. Educated by Clark and died in Oregon in 1866.

Drouillard, George - Hired as an interpreter by the Corps and was very good at Indian sign language. Killed by the Blackfeet Indians in Three Forks, Montana in 1810.

Sacagawea (also Sacajawea, Sakakawea) - Little is known about this Shoshoni woman who was born around 1788. She was about 12 when Hidatsa raiders captured her at the Three Forks. She was the second wife of Charbonneau and mother to Jean Baptiste. Died at Fort Manuel in December 1812.

York. - (No other name appears for this man) He was Clark's slave, who was raised with him. A big man and a good hunter! He was freed in 1811 and died on his way back to Clark in 1832.

Pg 58

Dutch Oven Salmon in Puff Pastry

Cod or Salmon Filet
Salt/Pepper ½ tsp. all purpose seasoning.
Pesto (Lemmon, Dried Tomatoes, Basil)
Frozen Pastry Sheets or Crescent rolls
1 egg

Remove skin and pin bones from the salmon filet rinse and pat dry. Bring the pastry to room temperature, about twenty minutes. Place pastry on a lightly flowered cutting board and pinch together any of the pastry that separates at the folds. Cut the filet into single serving size about 1-inch and a half (1 1/2). On the tail end you will want to combine two thinner pieces to keep the height the same. Place the salmon pieces on the pastry leaving about 3/4 of an inch sticking out from the salmon. Take the egg and separate about 1/4 of the white and discard. Whip the remaining white and yoke until completely blended. Add your Pesto topping to the topside of the salmon and cover with a second piece of pastry. Using the egg wash to seal the perimeter of the pastry and pinch down with a fork.

Warm your oven with 10 briquettes on the bottom in a circle around the base. Add 14–17 briquettes on the oven lid and arrange evenly to distribute the heat.

Place the salmon on the bottom of the oven and brush the tops of the pastry with the egg wash to give it a good golden color. Place the lid back on the oven and bake for 15-20 minutes until golden brown.

The smell will tell you when it's done.

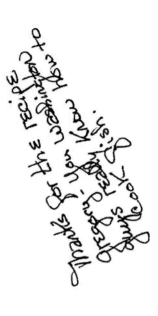

Thanks for the recipe. Gregory really enjoyed it. Let your mama know how to cook it. Linda

DEVILED EGGS

6 hard-cooked eggs
2 tbsp. mayonnaise
1/4 tsp. salt,
1/4 tsp. dry mustard

Make deviled eggs out of first 4 ingredients.

Serve with any fish dish.

April 7th, 1806 (Multnomah, Oregon)

"This morning early, the flesh of the remaining elk was brought in....we employed the party in drying the meat today, which we completed by evening and had it secured in dried elk skins and put onboard in readiness for an early departure"

Meriwether Lewis

HERB'S SALMON OR TUNA BAKE

1 1-pound can salmon or 2 7-ounce cans tuna, drained
1 tsp. lemon juice
1/4 cup butter or margarine
1/4 cup flour
1/2 tsp. salt
2 cups milk
3/4 cup shredded process cheese
About 12 pitted ripe olives
1 cup crushed potato chips

Break fish in chunks and arrange in a 12-inch warmed and oiled Dutch oven. Sprinkle with lemon juice. Melt butter and blend in flour and salt. Stir in milk. Cook and stir till thickened and stir in cheese. Pour half of cheese sauce over fish. Arrange deviled eggs and olives on top. Cover with remaining sauce. Sprinkle with potato chips. Bake at 350 degrees for 25 minutes or until hot. Use your Dutch oven in your oven or cook with 10 coals on the bottom and 15 on top.

LITTLE PORKY

3 pounds of Diced Pork
2 cans Cream of Mushroom soup
1/2 pound fresh sliced Mushrooms
1 box Pork flavored Stove-Top stuffing
1/4 cup of oil

Preheat 12" Dutch oven from the bottom for 5 minutes. Add the oil. Place the diced pork in the oven and stir until brown. Add the soup and mix with the pork. Simmer for 1/2 hour. Place Mushrooms on top. Prepare stuffing mix according to directions. Place on top of Mushrooms. Use 5 coals on the bottom and 10 on top. Bake 30 minutes.

This recipe is courtesy of
Richard Cowley
Author of Cast Iron Cuizine.

MARINATED HALIBUT STEAKS

handwritten note: these are like fish. Use lots of wine. Cast iron. Best

Combine:
1/2 cup catsup
1/4 cup salad oil
3 tbsp. lemon juice
2 tbsp. liquid smoke
2 tbsp. vinegar
1 tsp. salt
1 tsp. Worcestershire sauce
1/2 tsp. dry mustard
1/2 tsp. grated onion
1/4 tsp. paprika
1 clove garlic, finely chopped

Pour over single layer of 2 lbs. halibut steaks (1 inch thick). Marinate for 30 minutes at room temperature (or) overnight in the refrigerator. Remove fish, reserving sauce for basting. Cook over flame at medium setting about 8 minutes. Baste with sauce, turn and cook 7-10 minutes longer.

IRISH FISH STEAKS

Line the bottom of a 12-inch Dutch oven with washed and coarsely chopped celery, onions & parsley. Lay the 2 lbs. Fish steaks wiped Clean & cut in 1-inch thick pieces on top of the vegetables. (If frozen be sure it is fully thawed). Sprinkle the fish with curry, salt & pepper mixed together. Arrange on celery mixture, and place a slice of bacon on each piece. Bake uncovered at 350 degrees for 25 minutes in your oven. In a Dutch oven bake covered for about 20 minutes or until flaky. This recipe is good with Cod, Haddock, Halibut, Salmon' Bass, Northern pike or Tuna to name a few.
Serve with Lemon butter as follows. Cream together until well blended, V2 Cup butter, 2 tbsp. lemon juice, 2 tsp. chopped parsley, V~ tsp. salt & 1/8 tsp. pepper. Served with fish of any kind. Use with 12 coals on the bottom in your stoves, and 10 bottom and 15 top with coals only

BAKED FISH FILLETS

Follow basic recipe above, only substitute fillets such as cod, perch, and trout or flounder. Substitute tarragon for curry powder. Use same base and bake as directed.

IRISH STUFFED FISH

Use above recipe, but line bottom of pan with one thin slice of Snapper, halibut, trout or whitefish. Omit curry powder and put a layer of herb stuffing then another layer of fish steaks. Salt and pepper the steaks Bake for 40 to 50 minutes & serve with lemon butter.

SALMON SURPRISE

1 can salmon
1/2 cup cream of mushroom soup
1 1/2 cups soft bread crumbs
1/4 cup ketchup
2 eggs

Drain water off salmon and add water to make 1/2 cup. Mix the water with salmon and spoon into a warmed and oiled 10-inch Dutch Oven. Mix remaining ingredients together and pour over salmon. Bake at 350 degrees for 35 minutes in your oven at home. A piecrust can be placed in the bottom of the Dutch Oven if you prefer. Use 10 to 12 coals on the bottom of your Collapsible Volcano, and 10 on the bottom and 15 on top for briquettes only.

OKIE DOKIE SLICED BAKED POTATOES

Mm-mm good

4 medium potatoes
1 tsp. salt
2 to 3 tbsp. melted butter
2 to 3 tbsp. chopped fresh herbs, such as parsley chive,
    thyme, or sage
4 tbsp. grated Cheddar cheese
1 1/4 tbsp. Parmesan cheese

Warm and oil a 10-inch Dutch oven, Wash the potatoes and cut into thin slices but not all the way through. Put the potatoes in the Dutch oven and fan out slightly. Sprinkle with salt and drizzle with butter. Sprinkle with herbs. Bake for about 40 minutes Remove from the oven and sprinkle with cheeses. Bake for another 10 to 15 minutes until lightly browned, cheeses are melted, and potatoes are soft inside. Check with a fork. In your oven, bake at 350 degrees. With briquettes only, use 8 on the bottom and 11 on top. While using the Collapsible Volcano, you will use 10 or 11 on bottom, in a circle. No top heat is needed unless you want to brown the food.

DOVE AND RICE CASSEROLE

Chickens or Turkey may be used 39
= Versitle Recipe

15 doves or 6 Cornish hens
Oil
1 med. onion, chopped
2 cloves of garlic, finely chopped
1 tsp. lemon-pepper seasoning
7 cups rice
1 sm. can mushrooms
1 bouillon cube
Juice of 2 lemons
1/2 cup cooking Wine
Salt and pepper to taste

Brown dove in a small amount of oil in the bottom of a 12-inch Dutch oven. Set aside. Sauté onion in oil in skillet. Add remaining ingredients with 1 cup water; mix well. Arrange doves over rice mixture. Bake at 350 degrees for 1 hour in your oven at home. When using coals only, use 10 on the bottom and 15 on top. The Collapsible Volcano will require 12 in the bottom of stove on the lower grill.

QUAIL ON THE GREEN

1/2 cup margarine
8 to 12 quail or Cornish game hens
Garlic salt to taste
Salt and pepper to taste
2 cups sour cream
2 cans cream of asparagus soup
1/2 lb. fresh mushrooms, sliced
1/2 cup Sherry
Parmesan cheese

Melt margarine in a warmed and oiled 12-inch Dutch oven. Place quail in pan; sprinkle lightly with salt, pepper and garlic salt. Combine sour cream, soup, mushrooms and Sherry in bowl; mix well. Pour 1/4 of the sauce over quail. Sprinkle generously with Parmesan cheese. Arrange asparagus over quail; pour remaining sauce over asparagus. Sprinkle with Parmesan cheese. Bake in 350-degree oven until tender. The smell will tell you when it's done. That will be 1 hour and 10 minutes. Using coals, 10 on the bottom and 15 on top, and in the Collapsible Volcano, use 11 or 12 in a circle on the bottom.

Visit the Salt Works Memorial in Seaside, Oregon. The Corps harvested 4 bushels of salt here in 1806.

Substitute chicken pieces if you want.

HOLIDAY PORK CHOPS

4 thick pork loin chops
1/2 cup oil
1 garlic clove, minced Salt and pepper to taste
1 cup chopped onion
1 cup diced celery
2 cups diced unpeeled apples
1 cup water
1/2 cup Craisins, optional
1/2 tsp. each salt and pepper
3 cups Pork Seasoned Stuffing Mix

With a sharp knife, cut a pocket in the side of each pork chop. In the bottom of a warmed and oiled 12-inch Dutch oven, brown pork chops and garlic in 1/4 cup oil. Season with salt and pepper. Remove pork chops; set aside. In same oven, cook onion and celery in remaining oil until tender. Add apples, water, Craisins if desired, salt and pepper. Add stuffing mix; mix well. Stuff into pockets in pork chops. Place pork chops in the oven. Cover and bake at 325 for 1-1/2 to 2 hours or until Chops are tender. Using coals only, use 9 on the bottom and 12 on top. When using the Collapsible Volcano, use 11 coals on the bottom.

Sprinkle top with finely chopped red & green peppers before serving.

Breads Desserts & More

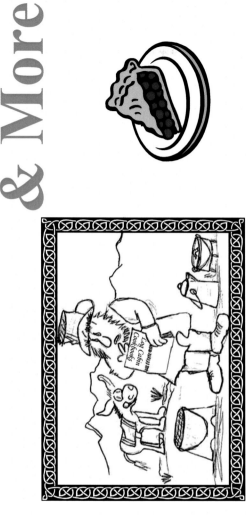

When they ask for Sourdough, I want to be prepared!

ALL PURPOSE BAKING MIX

2 cups flour
1/4 tsp. Salt
1 tbsp. sugar
4 tsp. baking powder
1/2 tsp. cream of tartar
1/3 cup oil
3/4 cup water or milk
1/2 tsp. salt

Mix it & use for Pancakes "Great Taste" so Good — #1

Mix all dry ingredients together and sift 2 or 3 times. Place in a covered container and use as needed. Add oil and 3/4 cup water or milk to mix as dough. If you prefer to use buttermilk, add 1/2 tsp. soda. It's a mix to keep on hand for easy biscuits for a meal. They can be dropped by tsp. in a greased Dutch oven and baked at 350 degrees in your oven at home. For low impact, back Country cooking; carry your dry mix in a plastic zip lock bag. Mix the wet ingredients in the zip lock bag for convenience. Using briquettes, 10 under and 15 or 16 on top for golden brown biscuits. Using your Collapsible Volcano, 10 on the bottom, in a circle, and turn oven upside down on the lid to serve. They will be golden brown on the bottom.

BANANA CHOCOLATE NUT BREAD

They came out once-great "Great Taste" — finally a banana bread in this [signature]

Dry Ingredients
4 cups all purpose flour
2 cups sugar
4 tsp. baking powder
1/2 tsp. salt
1-12 oz pkg. Chocolate chips
1 cup chopped nuts
Wet Ingredients
4 eggs lightly beaten
2 cups mashed ripe bananas
2/3 cup vegetable oil
1/2 cup milk

Mix all dry ingredients together in a bowl, set aside. Mix wet ingredients together. Add to the flour mixture; stir just until moistened. Pour into a well greased and warmed 12-inch Dutch oven, bake for 50 minutes at 350 in your oven, or until you can smell the chocolate, banana flavor. Cool 5 minutes with the kid off and loosen around the edges with a knife. Put the lid back on and turn upside down on a 4 in 1 trivet/Lid holder. Serve warm or wrap and store overnight if you can keep it from the family. Use 10 or 11 briquettes in your Collapsible Volcano. Using briquettes only, put 10 on the bottom in a circle and 15 on the top. You will have to replace the coals at least once.

Apple Crisp

Warm and oil a 12-inch Dutch oven
Peel and slice 8 apples
Place in Dutch oven sprinkle with next 3 ingredients.
1 tsp. Cinnamon, if desired
1 tbsp. Water
1 tsp. Lemon juice
Combine and mix in bowl,
1 cup Oatmeal
3/4 cup flour
3/4 cup packed brown sugar
1/2 cup butter, softened

Sprinkle crumb mixture evenly over apples, then bake at 350 degrees for 25 to 35 minutes in your oven, or until you can smell it. Serve with whipped cream. 10 to 12 briquettes in a circle in your Collapsible Volcano and 10 bottom and 15 top with briquettes only.

VARIATIONS:

Substitute blueberries, Peaches, Pears and Pineapple or any fruit combination your brain can come up with, for the apples. Fresh fruit is best, but pie filling will work.

Blackberry Cobbler

Filling:

2/3 cup sugar
2 tbsp. flour
4 cups fresh or thawed frozen blackberries

Combine sugar and flour in a bowl. Add the blackberries and pour the mixture into a 12-inch, warmed and oiled, Dutch oven.

To make the Crust:

1 cup flour
1 tsp. baking powder
1 1/2 tbsp. butter (chilled)
6 tbsp. milk

Mix dry ingredients together, cutting in butter until the mixture resembles coarse crumbs. Stir in milk to create a soft dough. Knead lightly until smooth and roll out dough to an 11-inch circle and place dough over berries. Cut slits in dough for steam to escape. Bake 20-30 minutes in your oven and wait for the smell. Use 10 briquettes on the bottom and 15 on top for briquettes only.

QUICK LEMON-WALNUT TREAT

1 can crushed pineapple
1 cup Powdered or brown Sugar
1 Lemon cake mix
1 can 7-up or mountain dew
1/2 cup chopped walnuts
1 12 oz. Cool whip

This one will really rock.
Satish

Start 10 or 11 Briquettes in your Collapsible Volcano with the damper open, or 25 in a charcoal fire starter. Lightly warm and grease your 12" Dutch oven. Drain the pineapple and pour into the Oven. Sprinkle the sugar over the pineapple and lightly mix in. Spread the nuts and dry cake mix over the pineapple. Drizzle the can of pop over the mixture and do not stir. Place heated lid on Dutch oven and place in Collapsible Volcano. Bake for about 25 minutes and wait for the smell. Steam will escape around the edges with the smell telling you when it is done. Allow cake to cool slightly. Serve with whipped cream or ice cream. Using briquettes only, 10 on bottom and 15 on top.

Most of these recipes are simple and designed to help you, the first time you Dutch oven cook. From that point on you'll want to try more sophisticated recipes. Any recipe in any cookbook can be done in a Dutch oven. I would suggest making your first Dutch oven a 12-inch oven and most any cookbook recipe can be cooked in it. Give it a try and you'll love it.

EASY SPONGE CAKE

6 eggs
3/ tsp. cream of tartar
1/2 cup Sugar
1 1/2 cups flour
1/2 cup Sugar
1/2 tsp. Baking powder
1/ tsp. salt
1/2 cup Water or apricot nectar or pineapple juice
1 tbsp. grated orange peel
1 tsp. lemon extract

Beat the eggs together with the cream of tarter, gradually add the 1/2 cup sugar beating thoroughly. Add flour, remaining sugar, baking powder, salt, water, and flavorings. Blend well, until thoroughly moistened. Pour batter into a warmed and oiled 10" Dutch oven and bake at 350 degrees for 40 to 45 minutes or until you can smell it. Loosen cake from side of oven, Invert on the greased lid and cool slightly before cutting. Use 10 briquettes in your Collapsible stove or Volcano. Be sure to keep them in a circle underneath the oven, and use 10 on bottom and 15 on top when using briquettes only.

This one is very good or with a fruit topping or cooled & frosted!

Don't forget the whip cream or ICE CREAM

May 28, 1805
"Our ropes are but slender, all of them except one being made of Elk's skins, and much worn, frequently wet and exposed to the heat of the weather are weak and rotten."

Meriwether Lewis

MISSISSIPPI MUD CAKE

1/2 cup Butter
1 cup Sugar
3 eggs
3/4 cup flour
1/3 cup Cocoa
1/2 tsp. Baking powder
Dash of Salt
1 tsp. Vanilla extract
1 cup chopped Pecans

FROSTING

6 tbsp. Butter
2 cups powdered sugar
1/2 cup Cocoa
1/2 cup milk
1 tsp. Vanilla flavoring

For frosting, cream butter in small mixer bowl. Add powdered sugar and cocoa alternately with milk. Beat to spreading consistency (additional tbsp. of milk may be needed). Blend in vanilla. Makes about 2 cups frosting. Cool thoroughly before cutting into squares.

Cream butter and sugar add eggs, one at a time, beating well after each addition. Stir in flour, Cocoa, baking powder and salt. Stir in vanilla and nuts. Spoon the batter into warmed and greased 12" Dutch oven, then bake for 25 to 30 minutes or until you can smell it. Use 10 briquettes in your Collapsible Volcano in a circle underneath. For briquettes only, use 10 on bottom and 15 on top. 350 degrees in your oven.

Is a Rum or Almond Substitute, Almond or Rum Natural flavor,

Would be great on a chocolate cake, probably be heavenly on a Baked Alaska, this

INDIAN CHARLIE'S PUDDING

4 cup milk, scalded
2 tsp. cinnamon
2/3 cup yellow cornmeal
2 tsp. ground ginger
1 stick butter
1 tsp. nutmeg
1 cup molasses
1/8 tsp. salt
1/2 cup. sugar
2 tsp. vanilla
2 eggs
1 1/2 cup cold milk

In the top of a double boiler, combine the scalded milk and cornmeal. Cook over rapidly boiling water for 30 minutes, stirring constantly. Stir in butter until melted. Stir in molasses, sugar, spices, salt and vanilla. Mix 1-1/2 cup of cold milk with the eggs before stirring eggs into mixture. Pour mixture into a warm and greased 2 qt. Dutch oven. Pour remaining cup of cold milk into mixture, but do not stir. Bake in a 300-degree oven 2 to 2-1/2 hours. Serve warm with whipped cream. In your Collapsible Volcano, light 6 or 7 briquettes. Bake low and slow. You will have to replace briquettes once.

HOMEMADE YEAST (OLD RECIPE)

Liquid yeast: Early in the day, boil one ounce of hest hops in two quarts of water for thirty minutes; strain and let the liquid cool to warmth of new milk; put it in an earthen crock, or bowl. Add 4 tsp. each of salt and brown sugar; now beat up 2 cup of flour with part of liquid and add to remainder, mixing well together and set aside in warm place for three days, then add 1 cup smooth, mashed boiled potatoes. Keep near the range in a warm place and stir frequently until it is well fermented; place in a sterilized, wide mouth jug or a glass fruit jar. Seal tightly and keep in a cool place for use. It should thus keep well for two months and be improved with age. Use same quantity as other yeast, but always shake the jug well before pouring out.

Dry yeast cakes: To a quantity of liquid yeast add enough sifted flour to make a thick batter, stir in 1 tsp. salt and set to rise. When risen, stir in sifted and dried cornmeal, enough to form a thick mush; set in warm place and let rise again; knead well and roll out on a board to about one-half inch thickness and Cut into cakes one and one-half inches square or with a two-inch round cutter; dry slowly and thoroughly in warm oven; keep in cool, dry place for use. Will keep fresh for six months. To use, dissolve one cake in 1 cup of lukewarm water.

CHINESE CHOCOLATE DROPS

Also Known of No-Bake Chinese Cookies [handwritten annotation]

1 cup semisweet chocolate chips
1 cup butterscotch chips
1 cup Chinese noodles
1 cup salted peanuts

Melt the chips in a warmed and lightly oiled Dutch oven, stirring as needed. Stir in Chinese noodles and peanuts. Allow mixture to cool and drop by teaspoonfuls onto waxed paper-lined baking sheets. Chill until set, about 15 minutes. Store in airtight containers.

July 22nd, 1804
"About 12, one of our men went out and killed a
large bear. We encamped at a handsome prairie on the
South side, opposite a large creek, called the Fire Prairie,
and which is 60 yards wide".

Patrick Gass

PEPPERMINT GUMDROPS

3 envelopes unflavored gelatin
1/2 cup Water
1 1/2 cup sugar
1/4 to 1/2 tsp. peppermint extract
Green and red food coloring Additional sugar
3/4 cup Water

In a small bowl, sprinkle gelatin over 1/2 cup water; let stand for 5 minutes. In a saucepan, bring sugar and remaining water to a boil over medium heat, stirring constantly. Add the gelatin; reduce heat. Simmer and stir for 5 minutes. Remove from the heat and stir in extract. Divide mixture into two bowls; add four drops green food coloring to one bowl and four drops red to the other. Pour into two greased 8-in. x 4-in. x 2-in. loaf pans. Chill 3 hours or until firm. Loosen edges from pan with a knife; turn onto a sugared board. Cut into 112-in. cubes; roll in sugar. Let stand at room temperature, uncovered, for 3-4 hours, turning every hour so all sides dry. Cover and chill.

CHOCOLATE PEANUT CANDY

1 pound white confectionery coating*, cut into pieces
1/2 cup chunky peanut butter
1/2 cup semisweet chocolate chips
4 tsp. half-and-half cream

In a microwave-safe bowl, heat coating and peanut butter on medium for 3-4 minutes or until melted; mix well. Pour onto a foil-lined baking sheet coated with nonstick cooking spray; spread in-to a thin layer. In another microwave-safe bowl, heat chips and cream on high for about 30 seconds or until chips are soft; stir until smooth. Pour and swirl over peanut butter layer. Freeze for 5 minutes or until set. Break into small pieces. Yield: about 1-1/2 pounds. Editor's Note: This recipe was tested using a 700-watt microwave.

* White confectionery coating is found in the baking section of most stores. It is sometimes labeled "almond bark" or "candy coating" and is sometimes sold in 1 lb. Packages.

PECAN LOGS

3 cup powdered sugar
1 jar (7 ounces) marshmallow crème
1 tsp. vanilla extract
1 bag (14 ounces) caramels
3 tbsp. water
1 1/2 cup chopped pecans

In a bowl, combine sugar, crème and vanilla; knead until smooth (mixture will be dry). Shape into six 4-1/2 X 1-1/4-in. logs. Chill overnight. In the top of a double boiler over boiling water, cook and stir caramels and water until smooth. Dip logs into caramel; roll in pecans. Chill for 2 hours. Cut into thin slices.

"This was Mom's specialty"

"My Dad always said that Christmas wasn't complete without Mom's special logs."

LOG CABIN SUGAR CREAM PIE

1/2 cup Sugar
2 cup Cream
1/2 cup Brown sugar
2 tbsp. Corn Starch
1 uncooked Pie shell
1/2 cup Flour
1/2 tsp. Nutmeg
1/8 tsp. Salt

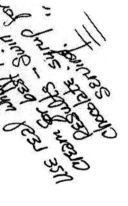

In small bowl, mix sugars, flour and salt. Gradually stir in heavy cream, beating well. Place in a warmed and oil 10-inch Dutch oven, as a bottom crust. Pour the mixture into the crust. Sprinkle the nutmeg on top. Heat Dutch oven lid and place on oven. Bake 20~25 minutes with 9 or 10 coals underneath in your Collapsible Volcano. When using briquettes only, 9 on the bottom and 15 on top. When using your oven, 375 for 25 to 30 minutes. The smell will tell you when it's done.

VARIATIONS FOR SUGAR CREAM PIES

Coconut Cream Pie: Stir 1/2 cup shredded coconut into cream filling. Cover with 1/2 cup coconut.

Raspberry Cream Pie: Lightly stir 1 cup raspberries into cream filling just before turning into shell. Serve with whipped cream or Ice cream.

Meringue Topping: In medium bowl, beat 3 egg whites and ~ teaspoon cream of tartar until soft peaks form. Gradually add 1/2 tbsp. sugar; Continue beating until stiff peaks form. Can be baked on top of cream filling.

On the way home

September 17th, 1806
"We received some civilities of Captain McClallan.
He gave us some biscuit, chocolate, sugar, and whiskey
for which our party were in want, and for which we
made a return of a barrel of corn and much obliged to
him".

Captain Clark

SAUSAGE APPLE PASTRY PUFFS

4 pkg. crescent refrigerator rolls or 12 to 16 pastry shells
1 lb. pkg. Maple sausage
1 1/4 cup maple syrup
2 eggs
2 large peeled and diced apples
1 1/2 cups dry herb-stuffing mix
1 tbsp. water
4 tbsp. sesame seeds
1/2 cup sliced green onions

In a large bowl, combine the sausage, syrup, eggs, onion, stuffing mix and diced apples. Mix well and set aside. Spread out the pastry sheets on a lightly floured plastic cutting board. Spread 3 or 4 tbsp. of sausage mix onto each pastry sheet. Fold over the sheets and crimp to seal the edges. Make 3-in.-long cuts in pastry to allow for steam escape Brush top with milk if desired to help browning. Sprinkle with sesame seeds (optional) and place in a warmed and oiled 12" Dutch oven. Bake at 350 to 375 for 30 minutes or until golden brown. The smell will tell you when it's done. When using the Volcano or the collapsible, 8 on the bottom and 15 on top. If using briquettes only, 8 bottom and 18 to 20 on top.

*"Good Breakfast.
Brunch idea.
Great surprise
for company."*

HONEY BERRY SHORTCAKES

2 cup baking mix (Bisquick)
2 tbsp. Cocoa powder
1/4 tsp. nutmeg
3/4 cup yogurt
3 tbsp. honey
2 tbsp. oil
2 cup sliced strawberries
1 tbsp. sugar
1 1/2 cup whipped cream

Combine baking mix, Cocoa and nutmeg in a medium bowl and mix well. Add yogurt, honey and oil, stirring until soft dough forms. Drop dough by large spoonfuls into a greased 12-inch Dutch oven, 1 inch apart. Bake shortcakes in oven with 8 briquettes on the bottom and 15 to 18 on top, about 15 minutes. Combine strawberries and sugar in a small bowl. Slice cooled shortcakes in half horizontally and place bottom halves on individual plates. Divide whipped cream and strawberries among shortcake bottoms. Top with remaining shortcake halves. Serve immediately.

*Any Berries can be used,
used in this recipe.
Blue, Black or etc.
Gooseberries with a little
add cinnamon are
good to.*

Double-Decker Confetti Brownies

3/4 cup (1 1/2 sticks) butter or margarine, softened
1 cup granulated sugar
1 cup firmly packed light brown sugar
3 large eggs
1 tsp. vanilla extract
2 1/2 cups all-purpose flour, divided
2 1/2 tsp baking powder
1/3 tsp. salt
1/3 cup unsweetened cocoa powder
1 tbsp. butter or margarine, melted
1 cup Chocolate Baking Bits, divided

Warm and lightly grease a 12" Dutch oven. Set aside. In large bowl, cream 3/4 cup butter and sugars until light and fluffy. Beat in eggs and vanilla. Mix in 2 1/4 cups flour, baking powder and salt; blend into creamed mixture. Divide batter in half. Blend together cocoa powder and melted butter; stir into one half of the dough. Spread cocoa dough evenly into prepared Dutch oven. Stir remaining 1/4 cup flour and 1/2 cup Chocolate Baking Bits into remaining dough; spread evenly over Cocoa dough in the Dutch oven. Sprinkle with remaining 1/4 cup Chocolate Baking Bits. Bake 25 to 30 minutes or until edges start to pull away from sides of oven or wait for the smell.

(handwritten note: "no comment this" / "we do for" / "please" / "these are great!!!")

Blueberry Streusel Cobbler

1 pint frozen blueberries
1 (14-ounce) can EAGLE BRAND Sweetened Condensed Milk
    (NQT evaporated milk)
2 tsp. grated lemon peel
3/4 cup plus 2 tbsp. cold butter
2 cups all purpose baking mix,
1/3 cup brown sugar
1/2 cup chopped nuts

In bowl, combine Blueberries, Eagle Brand and Lemon peel. In large bowl, cut 3/4 cup butter into 1 1/2 cups biscuit mix until crumbly; add blueberry mixture. Place in a 12-inch warmed and oiled Dutch oven. In small bowl, combine remaining 1/2 cup biscuit mix and sugar; cut in remaining 2 tbsp. butter until crumbly. Add nuts. Sprinkle over cobbler. Bake 1 hour and 10 minutes or until golden. Serve warm with whipped cream or Ice Cream, Refrigerate leftovers. Bake at 350 in your oven in a warmed and oiled 12-inch Dutch oven. For briquettes, use 10 on the bottom and 15 on top. In your Volcano use 12 coals on the bottom in a circle.

BLUEBERRY STREUSEL POUND CAKE

1/3 cup sugar
1/4 cup butter
1 egg
2 1/3 cups flour
4 tsp. baking powder
1/2 tsp. salt
1 cup buttermilk
1 tsp. vanilla
1 1/2 cups fresh or frozen blueberries

In a mixing bowl, cream sugar and butter. Add egg; mix well. Combine flour, baking powder and salt; add to the creamed mixture alternately with milk. Stir in vanilla. Fold in blueberries. Warm and oil a 12-inch Dutch oven and pour in mix. Bake at 350 for 25 to 30 minutes. Use 10 briquettes in you Collapsible Volcano or 10 on the bottom and 15 on top for briquettes only. When using your Propane stove, be sure to use a deflector shield between the burner and the bottom of the oven. Keep your flame on low and put 15 coals on top.

STREUSEL

1/2 cup sugar
1/3 cup flour
1/2 tsp. ground cinnamon
1/4 cup butter

In a small bowl, combine sugar, flour and cinnamon; cut in butter until crumbly. Sprinkle over cake.

7 January 1806

"I hired a young Indian to pilot me to the whale, for which service I gave him a file in hand and promised several other small articles on my return. Left Sergeant Gass and one man of my party, Warner, to make salt, and permitted Bratton to accompany me.

"Proceeded to the place the whale had perished. Found only the skeleton of this monster on the sand, between 2 of the villages of the Tillamook nation. The whale was already pillaged of every valuable part by the Tillamook Indians in the vicinity, of whose villages it lay on the strand, where the waves and tide had driven up and left it. This skeleton measured 105 feet. I returned to the village of 5 cabins on the creek, which I shall call Ecola or Whale Creek. Found the natives busily engaged boiling the blubber, which they performed in a large, square wooden trough, by means of hot stones. The oil, when extracted, was secured in bladders and the guts of the whale. The blubber, from which the oil was only partially extracted by this process, was laid by in their cabins, in large flitches for use. Those flitches they usually expose to the fire on a wooden spit, until it is pretty well warmed through, and then eat it either alone or with roots of the rush, shanataque, or dipped in the oil".

Captain Clark, Fort Clatsop

PUMPKIN PECAN CAKE

CAKE:

1 box spice cake mix
1 can (16 ounces) solid-pack pumpkin
1/4 cup butter
4 eggs
2 cups crushed vanilla waters
1 cup chopped pecans
3/4 cup butter or margarine, softened

FILLING/TOPPING

2/3 cup butter
1 package cream cheese
3 cups powdered sugar
2 tsp. vanilla
1/2 cup caramel topping

In a mixing bowl on medium speed, beat the wafers, pecans and butter until crumbly. Press into two greased and warmed 12-inch Dutch ovens. In another mixing bowl, beat Cake mix, pumpkin, butter and eggs for 3 minutes. Spread over crust in each pan. Bake at 350 degrees for 30 minutes. Cool in pans 10 minutes; Serve from ovens or invert on the lid. For filling, combine butter and cream cheese in a small mixing bowl. Add sugar and vanilla; beat on until light and fluffy, about 3 minutes. Thinly spread between layers (crumb side down) and on the sides of cake. Spread caramel topping over top of cake, allowing some to drip down the sides. Store in the refrigerator or serve immediately.

> 16 August 1804
> "A fine morning, the wind from the S.E. I collected a grass much resembling wheat in its growth, the grain like rye, and also some resembling rye and barley".
> **Captain Clark**

CRANBERRY ORANGE POUND CAKE

1 1/2 cups Butter
2 3/4 cups Sugar
6 eggs
1 tsp. vanilla
2 1/2 tsp. grated orange peel
3 cups flour
1 tsp. Baking powder
1/2 tsp. Salt
1 cup sour cream
1 1/2 cups chopped fresh or frozen cranberries

In a mixing bowl, cream butter. Gradually beat in sugar. Add eggs one at a time, beating well after each addition. Stir in vanilla and orange peel. Combine flour, baking powder and salt; add to the creamed mixture alternately with sour cream. Fold in cranberries. Pour in a 10-inch. Dutch oven that has been warmed and oiled. Bake at 350 degrees for 65-70 minutes. Cool in pan for 10 minutes; remove from oven and cool. In a small saucepan, combine sugar and flour. Stir in cream and butter; bring to a boil over medium heat stirring constantly. Boil for 2 minutes. Remove from the heat and stir in vanilla. Serve warm over cake.

VANILLA BUTTER SAUCE

1 cup sugar
1 tbsp. all-purpose flour
1/2 cup half-and-half cream
1/2 cup butter (no substitutes), softened
1/2 tsp. vanilla extract

7 October 1804

"A cool morning. Set out early, the wind from the N.W. Proceeded on, passed the mouth of a small creek, on the L.S. About 2 1/2 miles above Grouse Island, passed a willow island which divides the current equally; Passed the mouth of a river called by the Arikaras Wetarhoo, on the L.S. This river is 120 yards wide, the water of which, at this time, is confined within 20 yards, discharging but a small quantity, throwing out mud with small proportion of sand. Great quantities of the red berries, resembling currants, are on the river at every bend. 77° 33' 00". Latitude from the observation of today at the mouth of this river [heads in the Black Mountains] is 45° 39' 5" North. Proceeded on past a small river 25 yards wide called Rampart or Beaver Dam River. This river (Maropa) is entirely choked up with mud, with a stream of one inch diameter passing through, discharging no sand. At one mile, passed the lower point of an island close on the L.S.

"Two of our men discovered the Arikara village, about the center of the island on the L. side on the main shore. This island is about three miles long, separated from the L.S. by a channel about 60 yards wide, very deep. The island is covered with fields, where those people raise their corn, tobacco, beans &c. Great numbers of those people came on the island to see us pass. We passed above the head of the island, and Captain Lewis, with two interpreters and two men, went to the village."

Captain Clark

Peanut Butter Chocolate Cake

2 cups flour
2 cups sugar
1/3 cup baking cocoa
1/4 cup creamy Peanut butter
2 tsp. baking soda
1 tsp. baking powder
1/2 tsp. salt
2 eggs
1 cup milk
2/3 cup vegetable oil
1 tsp. vanilla extract
1 cup brewed coffee, room temperature

Combine dry ingredients in a mixing bowl. Add eggs, milk, oil and vanilla; beat for 2 minutes. Stir in coffee (batter will be thin). Pour into a greased and warmed 12-inch Dutch oven and bake at 350 degrees for 35-40 minutes or until you get a good smell. In your Collapsible Volcano, use 10 briquettes on the bottom in a circle. When briquettes are used, 10 on the bottom and 15 on top will work. Replace the briquettes at least once during the cooking time.

Peanut Butter Frosting

1 package cream cheese, softened
1/4 cup creamy peanut butter
2 cups powdered sugar
2 tbsp. milk
1/2 tsp. vanilla

Glazed Lemon Cake

2/3 cup Sugar
1/2 cup oil
1 tsp. Lemon peel
1 tsp. Baking soda
1 egg
2 cup flour
1/4 cup Lemon juice
1 cup lemon yogurt
2 tbs. Sugar

Cream sugar and oil in a mixing bowl. Beat in egg, yogurt and lemon peel. In small bowl, combine baking soda and flour. Then stir into batter just until all is moistened. Spoon batter into greased and warmed 12-inch Dutch oven. Bake 30 minutes or until you can smell it. **To prepare glaze:** In glass measuring cup, combine lemon juice and sugar and microwave 25 seconds or heat to dissolve sugar. Stir. Pour glaze over cake. This is excellent served warm. The Collapsible Volcano require 10 briquettes on bottom in a circle around the outside. When cooking with briquettes only, use 10 on the bottom and 15 on top.

SHREDDED WHEAT BREAD - 2 LOAVES

2 shredded wheat biscuits
2 cups boiling water
2 tbsp. margarine
1 package dry yeast
1/2 cup warm water
1/4 cup sugar
1/4 cup molasses
1 1/2 tsp salt
6 cups flour

Crumble shredded wheat into bowl. Add boiling water and margarine. Let cool. Dissolve yeast in warm water and add to wheat mixture. Add sugar, molasses, salt and flour. Mix well. Knead on a floured board until smooth. Place in greased and warmed 12-inch Dutch oven let rise until double with the lid on. Shape into 2 loaves, put back in greased oven and let rise again. Bake at 350 for 40 to 45 minutes. When using the Collapsible Volcano—10 to 12 briquettes in a circle on the bottom, none in the middle. For briquettes only, use 10 on the bottom and 15 the top. On the Camp Chef propane stove, be sure to use a deflector shield between the burner and the oven. The smell will tell you when it's done.

SHEEPHERDERS BREAD

Dissolve
2 packages active dry yeast in
3 cups warm water
1/4 cup sugar
   Add
2 tsp salt
2/3 cup shortening, melted & cooled

Let mixture stand in warm place, 10 or 15 minutes, or until bubbly.

Then add: 4 cup Flour and beat well with a wooden spoon. Stir in 4 to 5 cups more flour to make stiff dough. Knead until smooth and elastic. Lightly warm and oil a 12-inch Dutch oven. Place the dough in and turn to coat with oil. Cover with a well-greased oven lid that has been warmed. Allow dough to rise until almost doubled, about 25 minutes. Watch closely or it will rise and lift the lid off. Place on 10 briquettes in Collapsible Volcano, in a circle underneath, or 10 under and 15 on top for briquettes only. Bake approx. 45 minutes or until brown on top and when thumped, it sounds hollow. The smell will tell you when it's done. This makes one very large loaf. Remove from the oven and allow to cool. Bread is a little heavier than regular bread but also makes excellent toast

ONION CRESCENT PIE BREAD

Warm and oil a 12-inch Dutch oven.
6 strips of bacon, fried and crumbled
Drain off excess oil.
Melt 3 tbsp. Butter in oven
Cook 4 medium Onions (finely chopped) until tender

Set aside and let cool.
1/2 cup Sour Cream
1 tbsp. Flour
1/2 tsp. Salt
3 eggs
2 tubes refrigerated
Crescent Rolls

> *April 13. 1805*
> *At the distance of 9 miles,*
> *passed the mouth of a creek on the*
> *starboard side which we called*
> *Onion Creek from the quantity of*
> *wild onions which grow in the*
> *plains on its borders".*
> **Meriwether Lewis**

In a mixing bowl, beat the eggs and combine sour cream, flour and salt. Stir in the bacon and onions: set aside. Separate crescent roll dough into four rectangles per tube. Wipe Dutch oven clean with paper towel and lightly oil again. Pat dough into bottom and 1 inch up the sides, stretching as needed. Pinch edges together to seal. Pour saved mixture over dough cover with the remaining 4 crescent rolls for top crust and bake for 30 minutes or until you can smell it. Using 10 briquettes on the bottom and 15 on top will make your crust golden brown. Be sure to keep the bottom briquettes in a circle underneath.

THE EASY DINNER ROLL

1 cup warm water (105°F to 115°F)
2 packages dry yeast
1/2 cup butter, melted
1/2 cup sugar
3 eggs
1 tsp. salt
4 1/2 cups flour
Additional melted butter (optional)

Combine the warm water and yeast in a large bowl. Let the mixture stand until yeast is foamy, about 5 minutes. Stir in butter, sugar, eggs and salt. Beat in flour, 1 cup at a time, until dough is too stiff to mix (some flour may not be needed). Cover and refrigerate 2 hours or up to 4 days. Grease and warm a 12-inch Dutch oven. Turn the chilled dough out onto a lightly floured board. Divide dough into 24 equal-size pieces. Roll each piece into a smooth round ball; place balls in the prepared pan. Cover and let dough balls rise until doubled in volume. Bake until rolls are golden brown, 30-35 minutes. Brush warm rolls with melted butter, if desired. Break rolls apart to serve. The smell will tell you when it's done.

QUICK BEER BREAD RECIPE

3 cups self-rising flour
1 cup sugar
1 room temperature beer
1 tsp. Salt

Tests have shown that Coors Light gives the bread the best flavor. Warm and oil a 12" Dutch oven. Mix together the 3 ingredients and pour into the oven. Bake at 350 in your oven at home, for 35 to 45 minutes or until you can smell it. When using the Collapsible Volcano, 10 or 11 briquettes in a circle underneath. When using just briquettes, 10 bottom and 15 top. If you are using propane, be sure to use a deflector shield on the Camp Chef burners, with low heat and hug tin foil, or 12 briquettes on top to bake.

BISCUITS

1 1/2 cup sifted~ flour
2 tsp. baking powder
1/2 tsp. salt
1/4 cup butter
1/2 cup milk

Sift flour with baking powder and salt. Out in butter until fine. Add milk to the flour mixture. Stir until moist. Knead. Roll out. Cut in 1-inch pieces or use a biscuit cutter for shapes. Bake at 350 to 375 degrees for 25 to 30 minutes. You will be able to smell them when they are done. Remember no heat in the middle of the oven underneath. When using briquettes only, 10 bottom and 15 or 16 top.

EASY INDIAN FRY BREAD

Combine following ingredients

2 cup Flour
1/2 cup powdered milk
1 tbsp. baking powder
3/4 tsp. Salt
3/4 cup lukewarm water

Stir and knead dough on a floured board. Cover and let stand for 15 minutes. Cut up into 8 sections and roll out to 1 inch thick. Heat about 2 inches of oil in a Dutch oven. Watch the temperature to keep it at about 350 degrees with a thermometer. Then, with tongs, place sections of dough into the hot oil. Turn over when brown. At this point, butter and honey are great or jam, or roll in cinnamon and sugar. You can also frost with maple frosting or any flavor you desire.

◆ Be sure to visit Pompey's pillar on I-94 exit 23 east of Billings, Montana. The only physical evidence left by the Corps is found here!

SPOON BREAD

2 cups yellow cornmeal
1 1/2 cup hot water
2 tsp. salt
1 tsp. baking soda
1 1/2 tbsp. margarine, melted
3 cups buttermilk
2 eggs, beaten

Put cornmeal in medium bowl and add 1 1/2 cups of hot water. Mix well to be mush like. Add margarine and salt. Stir in milk and baking soda. Add eggs, whipping slightly. Pre-heat and oil a 12" Dutch oven. Pour batter in and bake for 20 to 25 minutes. For a novelty, put 6 or 8 aluminum balls in the oven before adding mixture. When you get the smell in about 20 minutes, turn the bread upside down on a greased lid. Remove the balls and fill the holes with butter, peanut butter, jam or etc.

31 August 1804
"The Sioux rove and follow the buffalo, raise no corn or anything else, the woods and prairies affording a sufficiency. They eat meat, and substitute the ground potato, which grows in the plains, for bread".

Captain Clark

SOURDOUGH STARTER

1/2 cup lukewarm water
1 pkg. of dry yeast
Mix well and add:
2 cups lukewarm water
1 tbs. sugar
1 tbs. salt
2 cups flour

Mix well, cover and let stand for 5 days in a warm place. Stir the mixture several times a day. To keep, place in a container (other than metal) and refrigerate. Can be used with any sour dough recipe.

NOTE: The most important thing to remember about sourdough starter is to put the starter out and allow it to work for at least four hours before use. Every time you use your starter, replenish it with equal parts of warm water and flour. Use your starter often.

POTATO SOUR DOUGH STARTER

3 Potatoes, diced
8 1/4 cups flour
3/4 cup Sugar
2 packages of Dry yeast
1/4 cup oil
3 tsp. Salt

Cook potatoes, Covered, in 6 cups unsalted water until tender; drain, reserving 5 cups cooking water. Cool. (Use potatoes later for baking bread.) To make starter, combine 2 cups flour, 2 tbsp. sugar, 1 cup reserved potato water, and yeast. Cover; let stand in warm place several hours. Add remaining 4 cups potato water and 1/2 cup sugar Cover; let stand in warm place overnight.

Next day stir starter; remove 1 cup. Add 2 tbsp. sugar to 1 cup starter; pour into pint jar. Cover; store in refrigerator until ready to use. To remaining 4 cups starter, add oil, salt and enough flour to make moderately stiff dough. Place in large greased bowl. Let rise in warm place until doubled in size, about 1 to 1-1/4 hours. Stir down. Divide dough in thirds. Place in warmed and greased 12' Dutch oven. Three loaves can be baked in 1 - 12" Dutch oven. Let rise until nearly doubled. Bake for 50 to 55 minutes at 350 degrees. To use reserved starter, proceed as before, except substitute 1 cup reserved starter for first cup potato water. Use 10 briquettes on the bottom in the Collapsible Volcano. Be sure they are in a circle around the outside edge. When using briquettes only, put 10 on the bottom and 15 on top.

♦ John Shields was the gunsmith for the corps and also a valued carpenter.

Sourdough Potato Doughnuts

Mix:
1/2 cup sourdough batter
1/2 cup sugar
2 tbsp. shortening
1 tsp. baking powder
1 1/2 cups flour + 1 cup potato flakes or 2 cups flour
1 egg
1/2 tsp. nutmeg
1/4 tsp. cinnamon
1/2 tsp. baking soda
1/2 tsp. salt
1/2 cup sour milk with canned milk or buttermilk or water
(Add 1 tsp. Lemon juice to sour regular milk)

Mix all ingredients together and roll out on floured board. Cut into any shape and fry in 350-degree hot oil. Roll in cinnamon and sugar or what ever you can dream up or frost with maple or chocolate frosting.

21 October 1805

"One of our party, J. Collins, presented us with some very good beer made of the pa-shi-co-quar - mash bread, which bread is the remains of what was laid in as a part of our stores of provisions, at the first Flatheads, or Chopunnish nation at the head of the Kooskooskee River, which, by being frequently wet, molded and soured".

Captain Clark

SOURDOUGH RANGER BISCUITS

1 1/2 cups sourdough starter
1 1/2 cups sifted flour
3 tsp. baking powder
1 1/2 tsp. baking soda
2 tbsp. sugar
1/4 cup melted shortening
1 tsp. salt

Place flour in a large bowl making a hole in the middle. Add starter to the flour hole. Add melted shortening and dry ingredients. Mix from the middle, stirring in enough flour to make a soft dough. Turn out onto a lightly floured board; knead until the consistency of bread dough or a satin finish. Pat or roll out to 1/2-inch thickness. Cut with biscuit cutter and place in warm greased Dutch oven coating both sides of biscuit with grease. Let biscuits rise in Dutch oven with lid on, for 40 minutes, or double in size. Then bake at 350 degree for 25 minutes or until you can smell them. If start is very sour, throw away and start over.

Place 2 or 3 coals on top of oven to help with rising process

BEER BREAD ALA DUTCH

1 12 oz. can of beer (room temp.)
3 tbsp. sugar
3 1/4 cup flour
3 tsp. baking powder
1/4 tsp. salt
2 tbsp. butter, melted

Mix all ingredients until sticky dough is formed. Let rise in a greased and warmed 12" Dutch oven. Smooth top of dough and bake at 350 degrees for 1 hour or until you can smell it. Brush with melted butter for last 10 minutes of baking or spray with liquid butter or oil. When using the Volcano or Collapsible 10 briquettes on the bottom. When using briquettes only, 10 on the bottom and 15 on top.

Note: Coors Light seems to have the best taste!

Cornmeal Biscuits

Good Orange Bread "white" from Biscuits

1 1/2 cup Flour
1/2 cup yellow cornmeal
2 1/2 tsp. baking powder
1/3 cup shortening
1/2 tsp. salt
2/3 cup buttermilk

Sift flour, baking powder, and salt into mixing bowl. Blend in cornmeal and shortening, then add buttermilk all at once. Stir lightly with fork, just enough to moisten all the flour. Knead gently about 1 or 2 minutes on lightly floured hoard. Roll dough 1/2 inch thick. Cut with 2-inch cutter and place in warmed and greased 12-inch Dutch oven. Then bake at 350 degrees for 18-25 minutes or until you can smell it. Using briquettes only, use 10 bottom and 15 on top. When using the Camp Chef propane stove, be sure to use a deflector shield under the Dutch oven to keep from burning the bottom and place 12 or 14 on top.

August 30, 1806
"I left them on the bar and returned to the party and examined the arms, &c. Those Indians, seeing some corn in the canoe, requested some of it, which I refused, being determined to have nothing to do with those people".
William Clark

Cheese Rolls on the Double

"The Sioux". We are with it..... deep

24 yeast rolls
2 cup yellow grated cheese
1 tbsp. melted butter
Parmesan cheese

Warm and oil a 12-inch Dutch oven. Place rolls in oven close together. Make a depression in each roll. Place cheese in the depression. Sprinkle with Parmesan cheese. Let rise until double in size. Bake 30 to 40 minutes over 10 coals in your Collapsible Volcano. When using briquettes only, use 10 coals on the bottom and 12 to 15 on the top. You may need to replenish the coals at least once.

This recipe may be made with Dutch Oven Sweet Bread. Center may be filled with jams or jellies, marshmallows. Chocolate chips, raisins, any fruit Pie filling, cinnamon and sugar, etc. May also be deep-fried. Use your imagination.

3 cup Self-rising flour
1/2 can or bottle of beer (dark beer brings a bolder taste)
3 tbsp. Sugar
1/4 cup butter
1/2 tsp. Salt

Mix flour, beer and sugar. Add more beer if batter is to stiff. Put in a warmed and greased 12-inch Dutch oven. Pour melted butter over top. Bake at 350 degrees for 30 mm, in your oven. You will know by the smell when it's done. When using briquettes, 10 in a circle under your pot in the Collapsible Volcano, and 10 bottom and 15 top when using coals only.

Return Trip

- June 29th, 1806

- On the east side of the Bitterroots the Corps discovered the LoLo Hot Springs. All the Corps enjoyed the hot baths that night.

Crust:
1 cup Flour
1/2 cup Butter flavored Crisco
Pinch of Salt
1/4 cup Ice Water
Flour to Knead

Filling:
2 cups Sugar
1/4 cup Heaping Flour
1 tsp. Ground Cinnamon
Dash Nutmeg
5 Apples, Large, peeled, and sliced

Cut Crisco into flour and salt. Add cold water and stir until a sticky ball forms. Turn out on a floured board and roll into pie-crust. Warm and oil a 12" Dutch oven. Place one crust in the bottom of the oven and put apples in the bottom. Sprinkle Cinnamon, flour, sugar and Nutmeg over apples. Place second crust on top and cut slits for steam to escape. Bake at 350 degrees using 15 coals on top and 10 on the bottom.

Irish Brownie Pie

1 cup flour
1/2 cup butter
1/4 tsp. salt
1/2 cup cold water
2 sticks butter
4 squares cooking chocolate (melted)
4 eggs
2 cups sugar
2 tbsp. Irish cream liquor
2 tsp. Vanilla
2/3 cup flour
1/2 tsp. salt
2 cups chopped pecans

Mix flour, butter and salt until crumbly. Add just enough cold water to form a crust. Warm and oil a 12" Dutch oven. Place piecrust in oven. Mix all ingredients together and place on piecrust. Bake 40 to 45 minutes. The smell will tell you when it's done!

Bandit Beer Buns

They'll steal your taste buds!

2 cups Bisquick
2 tbsp. sugar
1/2 cup beer room temperature

Mix together the Bisquick and sugar. Stir in the beer just until moist. Spoon into a 12" greased Dutch oven. Let stand for 15 minutes. Bake for 18 minutes.

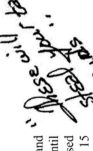

Lewis' Return

◆ July 27th, 1806

◆ Lewis and his men galloped across the prairie just south of (now) Conrad, Montana. This is the home of Doctor Dick Kinyon and family. Look them up it you're ever near by. They are great people.

APPLE PIE CAKE

8 large granny smith apples; peeled and sliced
2 tbsp. Cornstarch
1 tsp. cinnamon
1/2 cup chopped walnuts
1 tsp. nutmeg
1/2 cup Brown sugar
1 spice cake mix

This is a Favorite of everybody

Warm and oil a 12" Dutch oven. Mix cake mix as directed and set-aside. Put apples, walnuts, sugars, flour, cinnamon, and nutmeg in your oven. Stir until apples are well coated. Pour cake batter over top of apples and spread evenly. Bake at 350 in your oven and wait for the smell. Using coals only, place 15 briquettes top and 9 briquettes bottom in a circle. Never put coals in the center bottom of your ovens, you will burn the center every time. When using your Collapsible Volcano, place 12 coals in a circle and wait for the smell. About 45 to 50 minutes.

SNOWFLAKE COBBLER

1 cherry chip cake mix
1 can 7-up
1 large can cherry pie filling
1/2 cup Finely chopped nuts, your choice
1/2 cup Coconut
1 cup chocolate chips optional

Lightly warm and oil a 10-inch Dutch oven. Put the cherry pie filling in the bottom of the Dutch oven. Sprinkle nuts, 1/2 cup Coconut and chips over the cherries. Spread out the dry cake mix on top of cherries. Drizzle the can or pop over the top of the cake mix. Sprinkle the other half of Coconut over the mix. Place the lid on and put over 12 coals in your Collapsible Volcano. Make sure they are in a circle around the outside edge. When using coals only place 10 under and 15 on top. Then, in your oven, bake at 350 for 25 minutes. The smell will tell you when it's done.

This is a recipe my daughter made up by new. it's yummy! Lisa

PRAIRIE DEEP DISH APPLE PIE

8 apples peeled and sliced
1/2 cup Sugar
2 tsp. Cinnamon
1 tsp. nutmeg
2 pie crusts
2 tbsp. milk
1 tbsp. cornstarch

Lightly warm and oil a 10-inch Dutch oven. Place 1-Pie Crust in the bottom and arrange the apples in the bottom. Sprinkle with Nutmeg, Cinnamon, cornstarch and sugar. Put 2nd crust on top of apples and brush the crust with milk or egg wash. Bake at 350 degrees in your oven for about 40 minutes. In your stove, Collapsible Volcano, place 5 briquettes on the bottom and 15 on top. When using briquettes only, 5 or 6 on the bottom and 15 on top. This will brown your pie nicely. Be sure the coals are in a circle around the outside.

The following recipes are some from the
great cooks of the
International Dutch oven Society.
Try them! Some have even won contests.

THE GREATEST RHUBARB CAKE YOU EVER ATE

Mix together:
1 1/2 cups fresh or frozen Rhubarb
1 1/2 cups Brown sugar
Allow this to set aside for several hours or over night!
Sugar will dissolve!
Add:
1/2 cup soft margarine
1 egg
1 tsp. Soda
2 cups Flour
1/4 tsp. Vanilla
1 cup Buttermilk or sour milk

this was my Mom's very favorite to make.

Warm and oil a 12-inch Dutch Oven. Pour the mix into the oven and sprinkle top of cake with cinnamon and sugar and bake in your oven at 375 degrees for 25 minutes, or until you can smell it. In your Collapsible Volcano, 12 coals in a circle on the bottom grill an wait for the smell. When using coals only, place 10 on the bottom and 15 on top. Serve with whipped cream or Ice cream.

VARIATION

Add 1/2 tsp. Nutmeg and cloves

CARROT PINEAPPLE CAKE

Cake

1 1/2 cups vegetable oil
3 cups all purpose flour
2 cups sugar
2 tsp. baking soda
2 tsp. baking powder
3 eggs
2 1/2 cups grated carrots
1 tsp. cinnamon
1 cup crushed pineapple
1 tsp. salt
1 tbsp. grated orange peel
1/2 cup flaked coconut
2 tsp. vanilla
1 cup chopped nuts

Frosting

8 oz. brick cream cheese; softened
1 tsp. vanilla
1/2 cup butter; room temperature
1/2 cup crushed pineapple; well drained
3 cups powdered sugar

The Best Carrot Cake I've ever tasted.

"terrific"

Prepare Batter: In a large bowl mix together oil, sugar, eggs, carrots, pineapple, orange peel, and vanilla. In a separate bowl sift together flour, baking soda, baking powder, cinnamon, and salt. Stir flour mixture into wet ingredients then stir in coconut and nuts.

Bake: Grease and flour the bottom and sides of a 12" Dutch oven. Pour batter into Dutch oven and spread evenly to sides. Bake using 8-10 coals bottom and 14-16 coals top for 45-60 minutes or until toothpick inserted into center of cake comes out clean. For best results rotate oven and lid 90° in opposite directions every 15 minutes while baking. Allow cake to cool in pan for 15 minutes. Invert cake onto a cooling rack and finish cooling. Cut cake in half horizontally. Separate halves.

Prepare Frosting: Cream together all ingredients. Transfer 1/3 of the frosting to another bowl and stir in pineapple.

Assemble Cake: Set 1 cake layer on a plate cut side up. Spread the pineapple frosting across top of cake half. Top with second cake layer, cut side down. Frost top and sides with remaining frosting.

FRESH RASPBERRY PEACH PIE

Filling

1 cup granulated sugar
3 cups all purpose flour
3/4 cup brown sugar
1 1/2 cups shortening
1/2 tsp. ground cinnamon
1/4 tsp. salt
1/4 tsp. ground nutmeg
3/4 cup HOT water
8 tsp. instant Clear Jel
8 cups sliced fresh peaches
1/4 cup milk
2 cups fresh raspberries
2 tsp. almond extract
2 tbsp. lemon juice
2 tbsp. butter; cubed

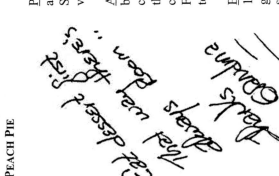

Prepare Filling: In a large bowl mix sugars, spices, and Clear Jel. Gently stir in fruit, extract, and lemon juice. Stir only to mix and moisten, being careful not to mash the fruit. Reserve the cubed butter.

Crust

Prepare Pie Crust: Cut flour, salt, and shortening together with a pastry cutter or 2 knives. Add hot water one half at a time. Stir with a fork just to moisten. Knead dough 4 or 5 times. Divide dough in half.

Assemble Pie: Place one piece of dough on a lightly floured board and gently roll out to 1/4" thickness. Place dough in a clean oiled 12" Dutch oven to cover bottom and 2-3 inches up the sides. Spoon in the filling. Dot the top of the fruit with cubed butter. Roll out the top crust and cut into 1/2" strips. Form strips into a lattice top over pie and seal edges with water. Brush top crust with milk.

Bake Pie: Cover and bake pie using 9 briquettes bottom and 16-18 briquettes on the lid for about 1 hour until top crust is golden brown and filling is bubbly. For even browning make sure to rotate the base and lid of the oven a 1/4 turn in opposite directions every 10-15 minutes.

Recipe courtesy of
Terry and Sheilamarie Lewis
of Tabiona, UT.
Another great recipe from
IDOS Dutch oven cooks

CHOCOLATE LOVERS DELIGHT

1 1/2 cup water
1 (10 oz. bag) miniature marshmallows
1/4 cup cocoa powder
1 chocolate cake mix; prepared as directed
1 cup light brown sugar
6 oz. semi-sweet chocolate chips

Line the bottom and sides of a 12" Dutch oven with heavy foil. Mix the water, cocoa powder, and brown sugar together and pour into the Dutch oven. Add marshmallows and spread them out evenly. Pour prepared chocolate cake mix over marshmallows. Sprinkle chocolate chips over cake batter.

Cover oven and bake using 8-10 briquettes bottom and 14-16 briquettes top for 60 minutes.

DUTCH APPLE CRISP

FILLING	TOPPING
10 cups granny smith apple slices	1/2 cup brown sugar
2 cups brown sugar	1/2 cup chopped walnuts (optional)
2 tbsp. lemon juice	1/3 cup flour
2 cups flour	1 cup butter; melted
3/4 cup sugar	2 tsp. ground cinnamon
1 cup oatmeal	3/4 tsp. grated nutmeg
	1/4 tsp. ground cloves
	3/4 tsp. salt

Prepare Filling: In a 12" Dutch oven add apples and lemon juice; stir to coat apples. In a separate dish combine remaining filling ingredients and stir to mix. Pour dry ingredients over apples and stir until apples are well coated.

Prepare Topping: In a separate bowl combine brown sugar, flour, oatmeal, and walnuts; stir to mix. Using a fork, mix in butter. Spread topping evenly over apples.

Bake: Cover Dutch oven and bake using 12-14 briquettes bottom and 16-18 briquettes top for 60 minutes. Serve topped with whipped cream. Serves: 12-14

CHERRY CHOCOLATE SURPRISE CAKE

1 chocolate cake mix, prepared as directed
1 egg
1 (#2 1/2) can cherry pie filling
3 tbsp. sugar
8 oz. brick cream cheese
1 tsp. vanilla

Pour prepared cake batter into a greased 12" Dutch oven. Spoon cherry pie filling into clumps over cake batter. In a small mixing bowl cream together cream cheese, egg, sugar, and vanilla until smooth. Drop by tbsp. over top of cake. Place lid on oven! Bake using 8-10 briquettes bottom and 14-16 briquettes on top for 1 hour or until you can smell the cake. Serve warm with whip cream as topping.

12 May 1805
"On the north side, the summits of the hills exhibit some scattering pine and cedar; on the south side, the pine has not yet commenced, though there is some cedar on the face of the hills and in the little ravines. The chokecherry also grows here in the hollow' and at the heads of the gullies. The chokecherry has been in bloom since the ninth inst. This growth has frequently made its appearance on the Missouri from the neighborhood of the Bald-pated Prairie to this place".

Captain Lewis

EASY PEACH COBBLER

2 (#2-1/2) cans sliced peaches; drained
1 can Sprite or 7-up
1 yellow cake mix and dry ice cream of your choice

Into a 12" Dutch oven add peaches and spread out. Pour dry cake mix over peaches then pour the soda over the cake mix. Stir to mix completely. Place lid on oven! Bake for 45 minutes to an hour using 12 briquettes top and 10 briquettes bottom.

June 3rd, 1805
"The chokecherry grows here in abundance, both in the river bottoms and in the steep ravines along the river bluffs. Saw the yellow and red currants, not yet ripe; also the gooseberry, which begins to ripen. The wild rose, which grows here in great abundance in the bottoms of all these rivers, is now in full bloom, and adds not a little to the beauty of the scenery. We took the width of the two rivers, found the left-hand or S. fork 372 yards, and the N. fork 200. The north fork is deeper than the other, but its current not so swift. Its waters run in the same boiling and rolling manner which has uniformly characterized the Missouri throughout its whole course so far. Its waters are of a whitish brown color, very thick, and turbid, also characteristic of the Missouri, while the south fork is perfectly transparent, runs very rapid, but with a smooth, unruffled surface, its bottom composed of round and flat smooth stones like most rivers issuing from a mountainous country. The bed of the N. fork composed of some gravel but principally mud".

Captain Lewis

SOURDOUGH OATMEAL BREAD

1 1/2 cup scalded milk
1 1/2 tbsp. active dry yeast
2 tbsp. butter
1 1/2 tbsp. sugar
3 tbsp. honey
2 tsp. salt
3 cups sourdough starter
1 1/2 tsp. baking soda
1 1/2 cup whole-wheat flour
1 1/2 cup white flour
1 1/2 cup oatmeal

Stir butter and honey into scalded milk, then add to sourdough starter. Stir in wheat flour, oatmeal, and yeast. Blend together sugar, salt and soda; sprinkle over top of dough and stir in gently. Cover dough with a cloth and let rise in a warm place for 20 minutes. Stir in remaining flour until dough is too stiff to stir with a spoon. Knead dough with heel of hand 100 times only or bread will be too dry. Dough should not be heavy and feel a bit tacky. Bake at 350 degrees.

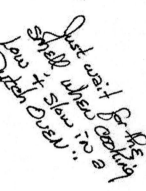

Just wait for the smell when cooking low + slow in a Dutch Oven

SOURDOUGH OATMEAL BREAD (CONTINUED)

Add dough to a lightly greased 12" Dutch oven and press flat. Lightly grease the top of the dough. Place lid on Dutch oven and let rise in warm place for 30-45 minutes.

Bake bread using 10-12 briquettes bottom and 18-20 briquettes top for 20 minutes then remove 4 briquettes from the lid and 2 from below and continue baking until bread shrinks from the side of the oven or gives a hollow sound when thumped on top, about 15-20 minutes. Tip bread out onto a wire rack and butter top.

If you'd like to know more about the IDOS, contact them on their web site, www.idos.org or write to them at;

IDOS
P.O. Box # 65767,
Salt Lake City, Utah 84165

Miscellaneous

Soups

Sauces

You're in the ARMY..... Now

The Lewis and Clark of Today

Veggies

Beans

ACE CAJUN MUSHROOMS

3 cups mushrooms, quartered
1 cup crabmeat (imitation Ok)
1/2 cup Sweet red peppers, diced
1/2 cup Thin sliced green onions
3 tbsp. butter
1 tbsp. thyme or oregano
1 tbsp. garlic
1 tbsp. Worcestershire
1 tbsp. Tabasco to taste (optional)
2 1/2 cup sweet cream
2 tbsp. chopped parsley

Recipe by
ACE Hardware Store
Pocatello, Idaho

In a warm 10 inch D.O. put 1 tbsp. butter and sauté the mushrooms. Set aside in a baking dish. Melt the rest of the butter and add the rest of the butter and add the peppers, onions, thyme and garlic. Sauté until slightly cooked and add the rest of the ingredients. Cook for about 7 minutes on high heat until the cream is partially reduced. Salt to taste. Add the mushrooms to the mixture and place the lid on the oven. Let simmer until the cream mixture begins to thicken.

This is a great crew of great people. Pocatello, Idaho

HONEY ONIONS

12 medium peeled onions
1/2 cup honey
Salt and pepper
1/3 cup butter
Ground cloves

Delicious Side Dish

Arrange whole onions in a 12 Inch oiled Dutch oven. Season with salt and pepper. Heat together honey and butter; pour over onions. Sprinkle lightly with ground cloves. Bake at 350 degrees for 20 to 25 minutes or until golden brown. Makes 12 servings. 15 to 18 Briquettes on top. (May be made a day ahead and refrigerated until time to bake.)

♦ Patrick Gass died at the age of 99 in 1870, being the oldest living member of the Corps.

His Journals are very interesting and not published until the 1900's.

BACON CARROTS

3 lbs. carrots (peeled and shredded)
1/4 tsp. pepper
8 or 10 slices bacon
1/4 cup snipped parsley
3/4 tsp. salt

Fry bacon in large 12 or 13-inch skillet until crisp; remove bacon strips, crumble and set aside. Toss shredded carrots in bacon drippings and heat. Season to taste. Cover and simmer for 10 Minutes on low. Sprinkle with bacon bits and fresh parsley. Makes 12 servings.

CABBAGE AND TOMATO SOUP

2 quarts cold water
2 onions
2 bay leaves
1 tbsp. salt
2 tbsp. vinegar
2 tbsp. sugar (or substitute)
4 tomatoes or 2 cups canned tomatoes
2 heads cabbage, chopped coarsely
4 or 5 lbs. soup bones or chicken parts, inexpensive beef or 4 or 5 beef and/or chicken bouillon cubes

Combine all ingredients in 12 inch Dutch oven; simmer until vegetables and meat are done. 14 briquettes in an Collapsible Volcano. 15 Briquettes on top and 10 under if you're using just briquettes. 350 degrees in your oven, or low heat on top of stove. If desired, finely chopped carrots may be added.

July 19th, 1804
I called this Butter Island, as at this place we used the last of our butter, as we approached the great river Platte.

William Clark

CALICO BEANS

1 lb. bacon
1 lb. hamburger
1 cup Catsup
1 tbsp. Vinegar
1 cup molasses
1 tsp. salt
1 cup brown sugar
1/4 cup mustard
1 can pork & Bean
1 can garbanzo beans
1 can kidney beans
1 can hominy
1 can Pinto Beans

Fry bacon in a 12 inch Dutch oven. Add hamburger & onion. When browned add rest of ingredients and mix well. Cover and bake in your oven on 350 degrees for 1 hour. When using the Collapsible Volcano, use 12 to 14 briquettes on the bottom. If using briquettes only, 12 briquettes on bottom and 12 to 14 on top.

Onion & Red Green Pepper's are nice addition

Add 1/2 tsp of Baking Soda & Vinegar to help with the gases.

CARROT PUDDING

1/2 cup butter
1 cup brown sugar
2 eggs
1 cup raw carrots, grated
1 cup raw apples, grated
1 cup raisins
2 cup breadcrumbs
1/2 cup flour
2 tsp. baking powder
1/4 tsp. soda
1/2 tsp. salt
1 tsp. cinnamon
1 tsp. nutmeg
1/2 tsp. cloves

In a separate bowl, cream butter and add sugar gradually. Add beaten eggs, grated carrots and apples. Add the dry ingredients. Pour into a greased, 12 inch Dutch oven, filling 2/3 full. Steam 2 hours. Bake at 275 to 300 degrees in your oven. Ten briquettes on the bottom in the Collapsible Volcano. When using briquettes only, 10 under and 13 on top. Bake low and slow, the smell will tell you when it's done.

This is one of my favorites especially with a Hot Rum Sauce + Ice Cream."

Uptown Green Beans

4 cups Fresh or frozen green beans
1/2 pound bacon, cut in small pieces
1 onion, diced
1 package Little Smokies, chopped
1 can cream of mushroom soup
1 jar Pimentos, chopped (optional)
2 cloves Garlic, diced or 2 tsp. powder

Brown the little smokies and garlic in 1 tbsp. Oil. Add all ingredients including beans and simmer 1/2 hour. Sprinkle with white or yellow cheese before serving.

Country Stuffed Mushrooms

20 medium mushrooms, stems removed (save)
1 lb. Italian Pork Sausage
1 package Cream Cheese
1/2 cup leftover rice or breadcrumbs
2 cloves Garlic, crushed

Brown sausage and mix remaining ingredients and stuff in the mushrooms. Cook for 15 to 20 minutes with top heat in a 12-inch Dutch oven.

Lemon "Oh My Gosh" Pudding Cake

1 cup Sugar
1/4 tsp. salt
2 tsp. Lemon rind
3 tbsp. Lemon Juice
3 eggs
2 tbsp. Butter, melted
1/3 cup Flour
1 1/2 cup Milk

Mix sugar, salt, lemon juice, eggs and lemon rind together. Beat well and add flour. Blend in butter and milk. Pour into greased 4-quart 10 inch Dutch oven. Bake at 350 degrees for 40 to 50 minutes. Arrange 10 briquettes in an outer circle in the Collapsible Volcano. Using briquettes only, 15 on top and 9 underneath in a circle.

October 8th, 1804
"The island is covered with fields, where those people raise their corn, tobacco, beans &c. Great numbers of those people came on the island to see us pass. We passed above the head of the island, and Captain Lewis, with two interpreters and two men, went to the village."

William Clark

COWGIRL APPLE PIE CAKE

4 cup thinly sliced apples
1 tsp. Apple pie spice
1/2 cup Walnuts, chopped
1/4 cup Sugar or 2 fists full of brown sugar
1 cup Flour
1/2 cup Butter
3/4 tsp. baking powder
1/3 cup canned milk or heavy cream
3/4 cup sugar
3 tbsp. Water
3/4 cup Sugar
1 egg

Warm and oil a 10-inch Dutch oven. Place the apples in the bottom. Sprinkle with 1/4 cup of sugar or brown sugar, spice and nuts. Combine the remaining ingredients to make a batter. Bake at 325 degrees for about 1 hr. 10 to 12 briquettes in a circle in the Collapsible Volcano. Using briquettes only 10 under and 15 on top. The smell will tell you when it is done.

CORNMEAL CORN DISH

2 cans Creamed corn
6 tbsp. Oil
2 eggs
2 small cans Green Chili's
1/2 cup Cornmeal
2 cups white grated Cheese
1 tsp. Garlic salt

Warm and oil a 10 or 12-inch Dutch oven. Mix everything except the cheese and chilies. Put layer of mixture then layer of cheese and chili's then layer of mixture. Bake in your oven at 350 degrees for about 1 hour. When using Collapsible Volcano, use 10 to 12 briquettes on the bottom. Briquettes only: use 10 on the bottom and 15 on top. The smell will tell you when it's done.

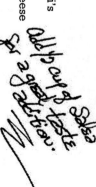

Use this Recipe if you want to catch a mate – Tasting! + oh- sooo good!

All 1 cup of Salsa for a great flavor.

Home Style Chicken Pot Pie

Best Ever

4 cup cut up cooked chicken
2 tbsp. butter
1/2 tsp. Salt and pepper
1/2 tsp. dried thyme
4 cup vegetables, diced. Carrots, celery, potatoes and onions
1 pkg. Frozen peas, thawed
1 can condensed cream of chicken soup, undiluted
1/4 cup dry white wine or chicken bouillon
1 refrigerated piecrust, at room temperature

Preheat 12-inch Dutch oven. Melt butter and chicken; sprinkle with salt, pepper and thyme. Cook and stir 1 minute. Stir in vegetables, undiluted soup and wine; simmer about 5 minutes.

While soup mixture is simmering, unwrap 1 piecrust. Using small cookie cutter, make several decorative cutouts from pastry to allow steam to escape. Top with piecrust, Brush piecrust with melted butter or milk. Arrange cutouts over crust, if desired. Bake pie 40 minutes or until you can smell it. Chicken mixture will be bubbly. Place 12 briquettes in a circle in the Volcano or collapsible stove. For briquettes only use 12 on bottom and 15 on top.

Sportsman Baked Beans

1 gal. Pork and beans
1 cup Brown sugar
1 cup Ketchup
2 1/2 lb. Bacon or Hamburger
2 large Onions
1 red and green pepper chopped
1 can crushed pineapple
1 tbsp. Worcestershire

Brown the bacon and onion at the same time. Pour off excess grease. Drain liquid from pork and beans, mix the rest together and put into a 12-inch Dutch oven and simmer for 20 to 30 minutes.

September 26th. 1804

"After a smoke had taken place, and a short harangue to his people, we were requested to take the meal, and they put before us the dog which they had been cooking, and pemmican, and ground potato in several platters. Pemmican is buffalo meat dried or jerked, pounded, and mixed with grease, raw. Dog, Sioux think great dish, used on festivals. Ate little of dog - pemmican and potato good. We smoked for an hour, till dark, and all was cleared away".

William Clark

COUNTRY DUMPLINGS

1 cup sweet milk
1 egg, well beaten
2 cup flour
1/2 tsp. salt
1 tbsp. baking powder

Stir all together and drop the batter, a spoonful at a time, on to boiling chicken or beef broth, or on soup and stews. Boil 10 to 15 minutes. These dumplings are very nice.

SAUSAGE DIP

1 lb. Country sausage
1 large onion chopped
1 red sweet pepper chopped
2 pkgs. 8 oz. Cream cheese
1/2 cup salsa, mild, hot or medium

Fry sausage onion and pepper until done. Slightly cool and add the rest of ingredients. Serve with crackers or chips. Can be done in a 10-inch Dutch oven.

This dip is great with chips, crackers or on Baked Potatoes.

TERRIBLY TASTY TARTER SAUCE

1 cup mayonnaise
1/2 cup sour cream
1/4 cup sweet pickle relish
1/2 cup ranch dressing
1 medium onion chopped fine
1 tsp. Lemon Juice

Mix all ingredients together and let sit 15 to 20 minutes before serving.

Thanks to <u>Herb Good</u> from Hood River, Ore.

Herb is a fishing guide on the Columbia River

CHEESY MUSTARD SAUCE

Mix together 1 pkg. Of cream cheese, 1 bunch of finely chopped green onions; 1/2 cup sour cream and 1/4 cup any style mustard you like.

Great sauce to liven up meats.

CREAMY HOMEMADE MUSHROOM SOUP

1 cup sliced fresh mushrooms
1 medium onion chopped fine
1/2 cube butter (5 or 6 tbsp.)
1 tsp. Salt
1/2 tsp. Pepper
4 tbsp. Flour
3 cup chicken broth
1 cup whipping cream

Melt butter in a 10-inch Dutch oven, Add mushrooms, onions and cook until onions are soft. Blend in the flour, and add the broth stirring constantly. Add salt and pepper, reduce heat and simmer for 5 minutes. Slowly stir in cream and mix well. Sprinkle sliced mushrooms on top and serve hot.

MEAT BASTING SAUCE

1/2 cup chicken or beef broth
1/2 cup finely chopped parsley
1/4 cup butter
1/2 tsp. Salt and pepper

Heat ingredients together and baste any meat wild or tame. This is great on wild fowl, tame chicken, turkey, Cornish hens or duck.

RED ITALIAN SAUCE

1 lb. Hamburger, sausage or both
1 can crushed Italian flavored tomatoes
1 tbsp. Garlic
1/4 tsp. Cinnamon
1/4 tsp. Allspice
1/4 tsp. cloves
1 onion diced
2 cup chopped celery
1 can roasted garlic sauce
3 tbsp. Butter
1 red and green pepper diced

In a 10-inch Dutch oven, brown the beef, onions and peppers. Add all remaining ingredients and simmer for about 2 hours on your stove.

> **Sergeant Ordway noted in his journal,**
> *"The meat (DOG) was cooked in a decent manner to treat our people with".*

Peanut Butter Bar-B-Que Sauce

2 tbsp. Cooking oil
1 cup finely chopped onion
1 minced clove of garlic
1 tbsp. Cornstarch
4 tbsp. Cider vinegar
1/2 cup water or white wine
1/2 cup maple syrup
1/4 cup molasses or brown sugar
1 tsp. crushed red pepper (optional)
1 tsp. Ginger
1/4 cup creamy peanut butter

In a 10-inch Dutch oven, heat oil and add onion, garlic and red pepper. Sauté until tender. Add the remaining ingredients except for peanut butter and stir well. Simmer for 3 to 5 minutes stirring frequently. Add peanut butter and cook for another 2 minutes stirring until melted. Serve with meat or brush on chicken or pork the last few minutes of grilling.

Barbeque Sauce By Jack

1/2 cup Jack Daniel's whiskey
1/2 cup Worcestershire sauce
2 cup chopped onions
1/2 cup cider vinegar
1/2 cup brown sugar
3 tbsp. Chili powder
1 cup strong black coffee
1 cup catsup
2 tsp. Salt
6 minced clove garlic
1 minced green pepper

Combine all ingredients and simmer for 45 minutes. Refrigerate between uses.

DUTCH OVEN SAUSAGE SOUFFLÉ

(From Log Cabin Low Impact Cookin)

4 cups bread chunks
1 cup cheese, white or yellow
2 cups chopped, cooked link sausage
6 eggs
2 cups milk or Half and Half
1 can cream of mushroom soup
1 can condensed milk

Warm and oil a 12-inch Dutch oven. Arrange fresh or dry bread in oven. Sprinkle on cheese and chopped sausage. Whip together milk and eggs and pour over the bread. Allow to sit for 1 hour. Mix can milk with mushroom soup and pour over the bread mix. Bake for 35 minutes or until you can smell it. Use 9 or 10 briquettes on the bottom and 15 on top for briquettes only. Use 10 briquettes in an Collapsible Volcano, or bake at 350 degrees in your oven at home. Be sure to keep the briquettes on the bottom of the oven in a circle around the outside edge. Waiting for the smell is the best way to tell when your oven is done.

*A great Breakfast dish
A great good all start's.
with read Plaese's guest.
Wilford Campbell*

This recipe comes to us courtesy of the Coeur d' Alene outlaws. Rick, Marci, Denny, Linda, Ron and M.J. Some great people who held their own cook out after a HERITAGE Class at 9-mile Ranger station in Huson, Mt. The joke was on Rick, cause Denny went around before the cook off and bought all the votes. They were a fun bunch.

CHILI ONION SOUP

1 lb. Hamburger
1 lb. Sausage
1 medium onion diced

Brown the above ingredients in a 12 or 13-inch cast iron fry pan and add:

1 envelope onion soup mix
1 tbsp. Chili powder
2 cans kidney beans
1/2 cup water
1/2 tsp. Baking soda
1 large can crushed tomatoes

Cover and simmer for 30 minutes. Serve with cheese on top.

May 23rd. 1806

"The child is something better this morning than it was last night. We applied a fresh poultice of the wild onion, which we repeated twice in the course of the day. The swelling does not appear to increase any since yesterday. The 4 Indians who visited us today informed us that they came from their village on Lewis's River, two days' ride from this place, for the purpose of seeing us and getting a little eye-water".

William Clark

JERKY

1 pound meat (any game will do--try duck as well as deer)
5 cup water
1 cup vinegar
Black pepper (1 tbsp. or to taste)
Garlic powder (1 tbsp. or to taste)
Salt - optional - to personal taste
Worcestershire, soy sauce, or Tabasco, etc. (approximately 2 tsp.). You will need a large pot for boiling a rolling pin a cookie sheet and a knife.

Cut meat into 1/2 inch or wider strips approximately 1/4 inch thick. Boil for 5 minutes in water, vinegar and spice mixture. Drain and cool. Roll each strip with rolling pin to remove excess water. If fluid is pink, boil longer. If clear or gray, it is ok). Place strips on cookie sheet and add Worcestershire or other sauce's) to taste. (Sprinkle or brush on). Cook in oven for 1 1/2 to 2 hours on low heat (200 degrees). Keep oven door ajar to allow moisture to evaporate from meat. Test meat by bending it. It should bend, but not break. If it breaks it is too dry so cook next batch for shorter time period.

Store in zip-lock bags or a jar in refrigerator.

Be sure meat is fat free

OLD WOODSTOVE BAKED BEANS

1 lb. navy beans (3 cups)
1 cup molasses
1 1/4 lb. salt pork, or chopped bacon
1 tsp. Dry mustard
1 cup chopped onion
1 tsp. salt
1 cup tomato sauce
1/4 tsp. pepper
1 1/4 cups cider vinegar
1 tsp. Worcestershire sauce
1 cup sugar

Soak beans overnight in water in a covered bowl. Drain off water in the morning. In a 12-inch Dutch oven, put 1/4 cup oil and brown the salt pork, add the onions lightly sauté. Add beans, and remaining ingredients. Cover and cook over low, but steady, fire. Stir occasionally. Do not let beans dry out. Add liquid if necessary during cooking process. This is easier done on the propane or home stove. On your Collapsible Volcano, 10 coals will simmer for 2 hours with the damper 1/2 closed. These beans can cook for 4 hours if necessary without becoming too soft.

EGG DROP SOUP

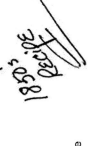

1850's Recipe

1 qt. water
1 cup peas, frozen
1 egg, beaten
1 cube Beef Bouillon
2 tbsp. green onions, chopped (optional)

Combine water, peas and bouillon in saucepan. Heat to boiling. Beat egg and drop into boiling soup. Simmer uncovered for 5 mm. Remove and serve.

24 May 1806
"At 11 A.M. a canoe came down with the Indian man who had applied for medical assistance while we lay at The Broken Arm's village. This man I had given a few doses of flowers of sulphur and cream of tartar and directed that he should take the cold bath every morning. He conceded himself a little better than he was at that time. He had lost the use of all his limbs, and his fingers are contracted. We are at a loss to determine what to do for this unfortunate man. I gave him a few drops of laudanum and some portable soup as medicine".

Captain Clark

Bite Size Appetizers

16 to 20 cherry tomatoes
1 cup or more crumpled bacon
1/2 cup mayonnaise
1/2 cup chopped green onion
3 tbsp. Parmesan cheese

Cut a slice off each tomato and spoon out the center. Place tomatoes upside down on a Paper towel and allow to drain. Combine all remaining ingredients. Mix well and spoon into tomato shell. Refrigerate until ready to serve.

Honey Sweet and Sour

1/2 cup ketchup
1/4 cup honey
2 tbsp. lemon juice
1/2 tsp. garlic

Combine all ingredients and cook over a medium heat for 3 to 4 minutes. Mixture will thicken slightly. Cool and serve with grilled fish or chicken. Takes about 15 minutes to Prepare & makes a great sauce.

Zucchini Scramble

3 small zucchinis
1 med onion
2 tbsp. butter
6 large eggs
1/2 cup grated cheese
3 tomatoes cut in chunks

In a skillet, sauté the zucchini and onion in buffer till tender. Season with salt and Pepper. Add eggs and stir till scrambled. Stir in tomato slices. Remove from heat and sprinkle on cheese. Cover & let set while cheese melts. Serve with toast or biscuits. You can add crumpled fried sausage for a great taste.

Try a cup cabbage & chopped this — with this Good Taste

Spanish Left Over Potatoes

2 cups left-over boiled Potatoes
1/2 cup left-over chopped ham
1 tsp. salt & paprika
1 tbsp. Chopped onion, green pepper & pimento
4 tbsp. butter or fat

Sauté onions, pepper and Pimento in butter until light brown. Add potatoes, ham and seasonings. Cooked till warmed through. Serves 4 to 6 People.

These next 4 recipes are courtesy of my friends in Boise, Idaho at Kampers Kettle. Mel and Jan Eggleston. Find them on the Internet and tell them "HOWDY".

OZARK BAKED CORN (12" DUTCH OVEN)

1 cup Cream Style Corn
1 cup Whole Kernel Corn
1/2 cup Corn Meal
1 tsp. Garlic Salt
2 cups Grated Cheddar Cheese
1 tsp. Baking Powder
1/4 cup Oil
2 eggs beaten
1 (4 oz.) can Green Chilies
1/2 cup Chopped Bell Peppers

Combine corn, corn meal, garlic salt, cheese, baking powder and oil in Dutch oven. Beat eggs in a separate bowl and add to mixture. Add chilies and peppers. Bake for 45-50 minutes or lightly browned. Place 6 charcoal briquettes on the bottom and 14 on the top.

ALWAYS REMEMBER TO PLACE THE BOTTOM COALS IN A CIRCLE.

CHILI EGG PUFF 12" DUTCH OVEN

9 eggs
1/3 cup Flour
1/2 tsp. (+ a little more) Baking Powder
1/2 tsp. Salt
1 lb. Cottage Cheese
1 lb. Shredded Cheddar Cheese
1 cube Melted Butter
7 oz. can Diced Green Chilies (drained)

Mix all ingredients well and bake at 350; or until eggs are set or knife comes out clean. Should take about 45 minutes. Remove half of the bottom heat at 30 minutes. Place 8 charcoal on bottom 14 on top. Serves 8 to 10.

WHEN COOKING EGGS, REMEMBER TO LIGHTLY WARM AND OIL THE PAN BEFORE COOKING TO KEEP THE EGGS FROM STICKING.

BOURBON BARBECUED CHICKEN

1 tbsp. plus 1 tsp. vegetable oil
3/4 onion, chopped
2 tbsp. plus 2 tsp. bourbon
3/4 cup plus 1 Tbs. barbecue sauce
2 tsp. lemon juice
4 boneless skinless chicken breast halves

Prepare 12" Dutch oven. Heat half the oil in a saucepan over medium high heat. Sauté onion 3-4 minutes in Dutch oven, stirring frequently, until softened. Stir in bourbon and boil 1 minute, until liquid is almost evaporated. Stir in barbecue sauce and lemon juice. Set aside. Brush chicken with the remaining oil and season with pepper to taste. Grill or broil 4 minutes per side. Brush with half the sauce and cook another 2-3 minutes, turning occasionally and brushing with sauce. Serve with remaining barbecue sauce.
Bottom heat only; 10-12 coals.

Thanks Mel,
see you on the cooking trail!

BEST EVER RUM CAKE

1 tsp. Sugar 1 to 2 Quarts of Rum
1 cup Dried Fruit Brown Sugar
1 tsp. Baking Soda
1 cup Butter
2 large eggs
Baking Powder

Before starting, sample Rum to check quality. Good isn't it? Now proceed. Select large mixing bowl, measuring cup, etc. Check Rum again. It must be just right. To be sure Rum is of proper quality, pour one level cup of Rum into a glass and drink it as fast as you can. Repeat. With electric mixer, beat one cup of butter in a large fluffy bowl. Add one teaspoon of sugar and beat again. Meanwhile make sure Rum is still ight. Try another cup. Open second quart if necessary. Add 1 eggs, two cups of fried druit and bead till high. If druit gets stuck in beaters, pry loose with drewscriber. Next sift three cups of pepper and salt (really doesn't matter). Sample Rum. Sift 1/2 pint lemon juice. Fold in chopped butter and strained nuts. Add 1 bablespoon of brown sugar—or whatever you can find. Wix mell. Grease oven. Turn cake pan to 3500 gredees. Pour mess into boven and ake.
Check Rum again and bo to ged

I think I had too much Rum while writing this one

Notes and a place for your own recipes

_____
_____
_____
_____
_____
_____

Log Cabin Grub

900 E. Carnation Drive
Sandy, Utah 84094
801-571-0789 (Home)
557-0798 (Cell)
801-495-0123 (FAX)

Please take a chance to go and visit along the Lewis and Clark Trail. There is so much to learn and do. Our SOLDIERS have fought and died to give us this Beautiful, Free Country. Start in St. Louis or anywhere along the trail for one of the most exciting vacations you'll ever take. My Grandson Adam has left for Kuwait to keep those FREEDOMS alive today, so I dedicate this book to him, my Dad, Dancer Davis and every other soldier who ever wore the uniform.

"Keep em safe Larry".

Pg 112